Easy & *Elegant*
LONE STAR QUILTS
ALL THE WOW WITHOUT THE WORK!

SHIRLEY STUTZ

Text © 2005 Shirley Stutz

Artwork © 2005 C&T Publishing, Inc.

Publisher: Amy Marson

Editorial Director: Gailen Runge

Acquisitions Editor: Jan Grigsby

Developmental Editor: Cyndy Lyle Rymer

Technical Editors: Helen Young Frost, Rene Steinpress

Copyeditor/Proofreader: Wordfirm Inc.

Cover Designer: Christina D. Jarumay

Design Director/Book Designer: Christina D. Jarumay

Illustrator/Production Assistant: Tim Manibusan

Photography: Quilt photography by Sharon Risedorph; how-to photos by Diane Pedersen and Luke Mulks unless otherwise noted

Published by C&T Publishing, Inc., P.O. Box 1456, Lafayette, California, 94549

Front cover: *Explosion*, Shirley Stutz, quilted by Martha Creasy

Back cover: *Spring Song*, and *Gone Fishing*, Shirley Stutz; *Jessica's Dream*, Becky Thomas

Library of Congress Cataloging-in-Publication Data

Stutz, Shirley Joan,

Easy & elegant lone star quilts : all the wow without the work! / Shirley Joan Stutz.

p. cm.

Includes index.

ISBN 1-57120-288-9 (paper trade)

1. Quilting—Patterns. I. Title: Easy and elegant lone star quilts. II. Title.

TT835.S766 2005

746.46'041—dc22

2004028545

Printed in China

10 9 8 7 6 5 4 3 2

This book is dedicated in loving memory of my parents, Frederick and Mabel Gunn, who among many life lessons, taught me to accept every challenge as an opportunity.

My gratitude is unlimited for the teachers, authors, publishers, guilds, shops and others who have fostered my love of quilting by sharing of their time and talents.
My heartfelt thanks go to:

My husband, Loran, who unselfishly supports and encourages my quiltmaking efforts, and devoted six months to the building of my wonderfully functional studio.

My children, Rick, Jeff, Doug, and Lora, for never doubting I could do this; also for understanding they must get on my calendar to find me home.

My very special grandchildren, Nolan, Rory, Amy, Kevin, Mitchell, Noah, Avery, Wyatt and Warren, who share their love and laughter, making our lives so much richer.

Rory Cox for helping with the organizational duties and record keeping for this book.

Cyndy Rymer, my talented developmental editor, who has been there every step of the way guiding my efforts; Diane Pederson, my Design Editor, who transformed humble examples into beautiful images; Helen Young Frost, technical editor, who made sure the book was technically correct; Gael Betts for providing understandable how-to photos, and all the staff at C & T Publishing for their diligent efforts to make this dream a reality.

Amy Marson and Jan Grigsby, who believed this book was worthy of sharing with the quilting world; Darra Duffy Williamson, who encouraged me for many years to put some of my teaching into printed word.

To my students who kept asking me when I was going to write a book; I hope I have not disappointed you.

My Elegant Lone Star students who offered to share their lovely work for your pleasure; the quilters who enhanced the beautiful stars with their needle skills.

My fellow guild members for their enthusiastic acceptance of my work; special quilting friends Jeanette Cox and Sheryl Hardesty for always being willing to listen; my sister Carol Lodge for "making" me take that first class; siblings Avonnah Cox and Alvin Gunn for encouragement to Œfinish, this book; Joanne Winn and Marlies Brandt, my go-to quilters for sharing their ideas and expertise;

Glendola Pryor, who insisted I begin teaching, and to Linda Mitchell, Sandy Heminger, Denise Guthrie, Effie Townsend, Cathy Daum, Karen Conley, Chris Konovsky and Maxine Holmes for offering so many of my classes in their shops.

Table of

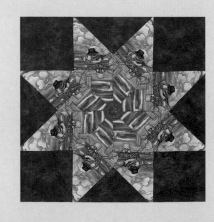

Contents

CHAPTER 1

Introduction

Inspiration, 80″ × 80″, machine pieced and quilted by the author.

Have you ever owned a piece of fabric that was just too beautiful to cut into? For several years my collection of large-scale, elegant fabrics had grown to enormous proportions, but I had not cut into one single piece. While working with various sizes of eight-pointed star blocks, I noticed my tendency to keep pushing the block size larger. I kept the area within the block interesting by cutting diamonds with identical designs. After completing a beautiful quilt created with of six 32″ eight-pointed star blocks, I wondered what a one block, eight-pointed star quilt would look like.

***Pink Splendor,* 78″ × 104″,** machine pieced and quilted by the author.

One-Block Quilts: Easy and Elegant

I sprinted over to my "special stash" fabric to select a really large print. Since this would be an experimental project, I pulled my least favorite fabric from the stack before me. The piece included both very large paisley elements and 8″ flowers.

First fabric selection

The next step was to draw a large diamond. I arbitrarily chose 20″ for the length of each side of the diamond. Working on newsprint, I quickly drew my template. I didn't wait to draw the two background pieces—a square and a triangle—but instead began cutting large fabric diamonds. As each diamond was lined up exactly on the print as the one before, cut, then placed on the design wall, the new pattern began to emerge. It was unbelievable. My least favorite fabric was transformed into an incredible design right before my eyes.

How exciting to realize that I had found a very easy way to produce an incredibly elegant quilt from just eight diamonds, four squares, and four triangles. Here was a way for quilters to finally cut into those wonderful large-print fabrics without destroying the beauty of the fabric. With this technique, new designs will always evolve within the star making it possible to create a truly elegant quilt using simple, large-scale templates.

With just one block per quilt, would all the quilts look alike? On the contrary, each quilt develops its own personality, with unlimited options for borders, plus many background piecing and appliqué options. In experiments with this pattern, no two quilts are alike in any way. Even when I cut sixteen diamonds exactly alike, the two quilts are vastly different if the diamonds are reversed.

Fabric used in twin quilts

Twin Number 1, 89″ x 89″, machine pieced by the author, quilted by Vickie Yanik.

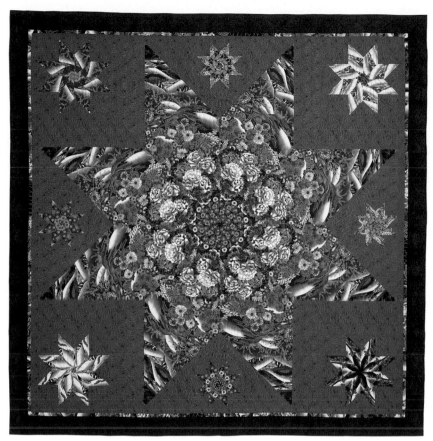

Twin Number 2, 86″ x 86″, machine pieced by the author, quilted by Vickie Yanik.

The size of the central one-star block in my quilts ranges from 65″ to 90″. The size of the three pattern pieces requires some special care in cutting and piecing, which is detailed in Chapters 4 and 5.

When I made *Twin Number 1,* I just cut the pieces, sewed the quilt together, and then measured to see how large the quilt block was. Quilters want to know how to make a specific size quilt, so the step-by-step process to determine the template sizes is an integral part of this book. Charts are also included, based on every 5″, for those who shy away from doing the math to determine appropriate sizes. A system for drawing accurate templates using ordinary quilting tools is explained. For your convenience, the pullout section has full-sized pattern pieces to trace.

Take your time to learn the whole process on your first Elegant Lone Star quilt. The second quilt will require just two hours to cut, and two hours to piece the entire one-block quilt. Amazing!

There are many tips for fabric selection, cutting with accuracy, and piecing the block using a no set-in seams technique. Projects offer background piecing choices and varied border options.

Teaching Elegant Lone Stars the past five years has convinced me this is not a pattern to be made only once. The search for appropriate large-scale prints from which to construct new and different Elegant Lone Star quilts has just begun. You will constantly hunt for any kind of print with a large motif: flowers, leaves, fish, animals, and more. Each time you cut one of these wonderful prints, you will become the creator of a new and exciting design. Enjoy the journey!

2

Choose Your Star Size

Snakes Alive, 94″ × 94″, machine pieced and quilted by the author.

Size the Quilt

The Elegant Lone Star quilt is one giant eight-pointed star block. The first choice to make is deciding the block size you want. The size of this quilt block plus any borders determines the total quilt size. Then you will need to make a few calculations for template size.

Some considerations to make in determining block size are:

1. What size do you want the final quilt to be? What size bed will this quilt be used on? Either measure your mattress top, or refer to Mattress Sizes on page 17.

Would you prefer to make a wallhanging rather than a bed-size quilt? Instructions are included for an Elegant Lone Star wallhanging in several sizes in Projects, pages 68 to 94.

2. Do you want the star to be contained on top of the bed, or would you like parts of the star to drop over the edges? (I think the star looks skimpy if it is contained only on the top of bed.)

3. Do you want to add borders?

The one-block star is very large, making the addition of several wide borders an appropriate option. First, think how large you want the finished quilt to be, such as 100˝. Deduct the width of the borders, such as 12˝ on each side, which results in a star block size of 76˝ (100˝ minus 24˝=76˝).

The eight-pointed star block is square. If equal borders are added to the top, bottom, and sides, the finished quilt will be square. If you prefer a rectangular quilt, this must be handled by adding a pillow tuck, or another innovative option to lengthen the quilt.

It is a good idea to photocopy the calculation pages (pages 12-17) so measurements can be kept separate for each Lone Star quilt you make.

Simple Math

A. Quilt Block Size _____
(the central one-block 8-pointed star)

B. Divide Quilt Block Size from Step A by 3.41.

_____

C. Round up answer from Step B up to the nearest ¼˝.

_____

For help in changing a decimal to a fraction, see the chart below.

DECIMAL/FRACTION EQUIVALENTS	
.125	⅛˝
.250	²⁄₈˝ (¼˝)
.375	⅜˝
.500	⁴⁄₈˝ (½˝)
.625	⅝˝
.750	⁶⁄₈˝ (¾˝)
.875	⅞˝

The answer from C is rounded up to the next ¼˝ to a user-friendly number that can be found on a rotary ruler. This rounding will cause the final measurement of the quilt block to be slightly different from the size listed in A by an amount not greater than ¾˝. To verify the final finished size of your block, refer to the Chart of Pattern Piece Sizes on page 17.

The answer in C is a very important number: It represents the finished length of each side of the diamond, the square, and the short side of the triangle, which are the three templates used to make an Elegant Lone Star quilt.

Record Keeping

Record your answer from Step C on the calculation pages for Diamonds, page 12; Squares, page 15; and Triangles, page 16.

Draw the Diamond Template

Tools and supplies needed for drawing include:

1. 24″ × 6″ rotary cutting ruler with 45° line marking.

2. Pattern-making material. I prefer Pattern Ease pattern maker by HTC because it produces the most desirable template. It is nonwoven, doesn't stretch, and is the easiest to see through. Since it is not ruled or dotted, there is no visual obstruction when you use it on your focus fabric. If it becomes wrinkled or creased, it can be pressed flat using a warm, not hot, iron.

3. Fine lead pencil or a permanent fineline pen.

4. ¼″ masking tape. Eight large diamonds are needed for an Elegant Lone Star quilt. Follow these steps to draw the diamond template.

1. Draw Line 1 the exact length determined in Step C, page 11.

Begin drawing Line 1 approximately ½″ from the bottom edge of the pattern maker, and ¾″ from the right edge.

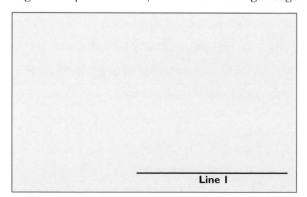

Draw Line 1.

2. Position the 24″ ruler with the 45° line on Line 1, placing the long edge of the ruler exactly at the right end of Line 1. Draw Line 2 the same length as Line 1, making sure it extends from the right end of Line 1.

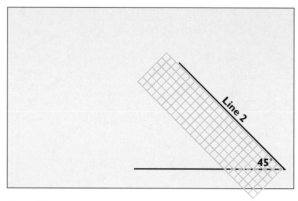

Draw Line 2.

3. Move the ruler to the opposite end of Line 1, with the 45° line over Line 1 and the left edge of the ruler at the left end of Line 1. Draw Line 3 parallel to Line 2, and the same length as Line 1. Measure Line 3 to make sure it is the same length as Lines 1 and 2.

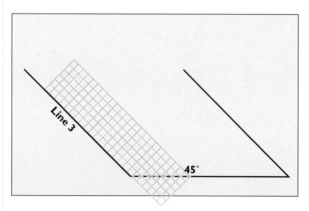

Draw Line 3.

4. Finish the shape by drawing Line 4 from the end of Line 2 to the end of Line 3. To ensure the diamond is perfectly drawn, align the ruler's 45° line on top of Line 2, turning the ruler over, if necessary. If the top edge of the ruler does not align perfectly with the end of Line 3, recheck your measurements and correct the drawing as needed.

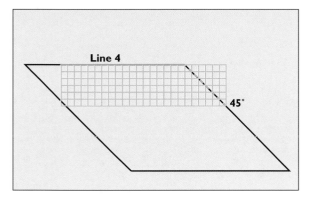

Draw Line 4.

5. To cut the pattern maker, place the ruler so the ¼″ line is exactly on top of the drawn lines. Use the ruler to add a ¼″ seam allowance while cutting the diamond.

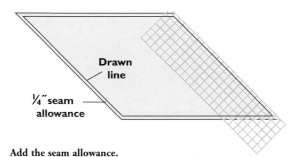

Add the seam allowance.

6. To check the accuracy of the template, fold it in half at the side angles, or what I refer to as the "elbows." The template will now be the shape of a triangle. The "skinny" points should line up on top of each other exactly; points will form at both sides. This step ensures that both halves of the diamond are exactly the same.

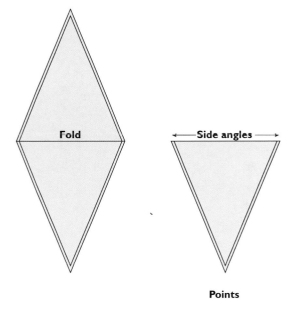

Fold and check for accuracy.

7. Place ¼″ masking tape on the outside edges of the diamond template, covering the seam allowance. Extend the tape a bit at the angles. Be careful not to stretch the tape. Stretched tape causes the template to ruffle and/or pucker, resulting in distortions. Discard any tape that is stretched, and begin with a new piece. Trim the tape at the angles of the diamond.

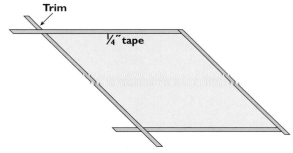

Tape the seam allowances.

Magnificent Macaws, 101″ x 101″,
machine pieced, appliqued, and quilted by
Sharon Gostlin. A lively jungle print makes
this quilt sing. Focus fabric designs were
used for Broderie Perse appliqué, checkerboard border, corner stars, and long sections
of straight borders.

Tape the seam allowance to block the view of the fabric in that area when you do the selective cutting. When a taped template is placed on the focus fabric, "what you see is what you get" after the star is pieced together. This prevents any unwanted surprises in the pieced area.

Taping also protects the template edges, and taped edges are more visible through the ruler when cutting fabric pieces.

8. Template identification: Record the finished size of the quilt block (see Item A, page 11), the number to cut, and the length of the lines on the template.

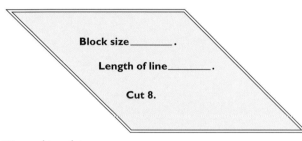

Block size_____.

Length of line_____.

Cut 8.

Diamond template

Draw the Square Template

Only 4 setting squares are needed for an Elegant Lone Star block! Prepare the template for your desired quilt block size by following these steps.

It may seem unnecessary to prepare a template for a square, but I highly recommend it. It is more accurate and faster to cut this very large square of fabric with a template.

1. Size of the finished square from Step C, page 11.

2. Add ½″ seam allowance. C + ½″ = _____

The template will be drawn with the seam allowance included.

3. Add the numbers from Steps 1 and 2. _____
This number represents the unfinished size of the template, including seam allowance.

4. Measure and draw the lines to complete a square on a piece of pattern making material. Each side will be the size determined in Step 3. Seam allowance is included.

Option: ¼″ masking tape may be applied to the seam allowances, if desired. The visibility of the template under the ruler is improved if tape is added, and the template edges are more stable.

5. Template identification: Record the block size, finished size of the square, the drawn (unfinished) size of the square, and number to cut.

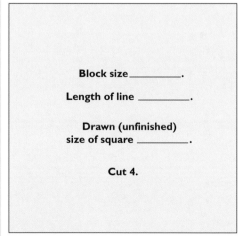

Block size_____.

Length of line _____.

Drawn (unfinished) size of square _____.

Cut 4.

Square template

Draw the Triangle Template

Only four setting triangles are needed for each Elegant Lone Star block. Prepare the template for your desired quilt block size by following these steps.

1. Length of short side of triangle from Item C, page 11. _____

2. Multiply entry in Step 1 by 1.414. _____

Note: 1.414 represents the ratio of the short side of the triangle to the long side of triangle.

3. Round up your answer from Step 2 to the next higher ⅛″. _____

This will be a user-friendly number that can be found on your rotary ruler.

The chart of Decimal/Fraction Equivalents on page 11 is helpful in making the conversion from a decimal to a fraction.

4. Add 1¼″ seam allowance for a quarter-square triangle. _____

A quarter-square triangle is used so the straight of grain will be on the long edge of the triangle, which is the outside edge of the block. This will keep the outside of the block from stretching.

5. Add 3 and 4. This is the triangle baseline. _____

6. Draw Line 1 from Step 5 on the pattern making material. Position the line near the bottom edge of the piece.

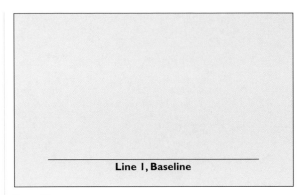
Draw Line 1.

7. Lay the 24″ ruler on Line 1 with the 45° line directly over Line 1, and the long edge of the ruler at the right end of Line 1. Draw Line 2 as shown. Draw a line long enough to pass the center of Line 1.

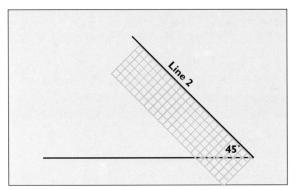
Draw Line 2.

8. To finish the shape, move the ruler to the opposite end of Line 2 and align the 45° line directly on top of Line 1, turning the ruler over, if necessary. Draw Line 3 as shown. When Line 2 and Line 3 intersect, the triangle is complete, and includes the correct seam allowance. Mark an arrow on the long edge of the triangle to indicate the straight of grain line.

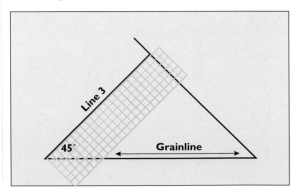
Draw Line 3.

9. Template identification: Record the block size, number to cut, and baseline length.

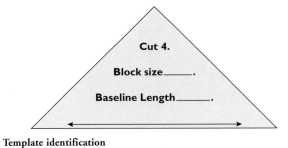

Cut 4.

Block size_____.

Baseline Length_____.

Template identification

Chart of Pattern Piece Sizes

Use this chart to determine the sizes of your pattern pieces. (You can also use it to find what size of block a specific size of diamond would make.) First, find the desired size block in the first column. The other columns list the sizes for the pattern pieces. Enter the measurements for the block size, diamonds, squares, and triangles on your calculations page.

Finished Block Size
(Complete before proceeding to Cutting)

1. Size of finished square from Step 1, page 15.

_____

2. Size of finished square from above. (Record a second time.)

_____

3. Size of long side of finished triangle from Step 3, page 16.

_____

4. Finished Size of Lone Star Quilt Block. Add 1, 2, and 3.

_____

CHART OF MATTRESS SIZES

MATTRESS SIZES	WIDTH	LENGTH
Twin	39″	75″
Double	54″	75″
Queen	60″	80″
King	76″	80″

ELEGANT LONE STAR PATTERN PIECE SIZES

DESIRED SIZE	FINAL BLOCK	DIAMOND No Seam Allowance	SQUARE with Seam Allowance	TRIANGLE with Seam Allowance
90″	90½″	26½″	27″	38¾″
85″	85⅜″	25″	25½″	36⅝″
80″	80¼″	23½″	24″	34½″
75″	75⅛″	22″	22½″	32⅜″
70″	70⅞″	20¾″	21¼″	30⅝″
65″	65¾″	19¼″	19¾″	28½″
60″	60⅝″	17¾″	18¼″	26⅜″
55″	55½″	16¼″	16¾″	24¼″
50″	50⅜″	14¾″	15¼″	22⅛″

Enchantment, 77″ x 77″, machine pieced by Debbie Arden, machine quilted by Martha Creasy. Debbie cut diamonds to give the cranes an important place in the diamonds. The intense contrast of black design elements shows off the lovely floral center design.

Radiant Garland, 102″ × 115″, machine pieced by Jeanette Cox, hand quilted by Rita Brownrigg. The fabric used in this quilt is the same as in ***Eleanor's Elegant Star*** (page 20) and ***Fantasia Night Star*** (page 79).

Eleanor's Elegant Star, 96¼″ x 104″, machine pieced by Eleanor McCanna, machine quilted by Linda McCuean. The same elegant fabric used in Fantasia Night Star and Radiant Garland (pages 79 and 19) looks entirely different cut from a different section of the focus fabric. Prairie points form an interesting inner border.

Kaleidoscope of Stars, 113″ x 113″, machine pieced and quilted by Patty Howells. Unique center shapes were cut from the focus fabric, which was also used for both outer sashing and stars in the outer border.

Supplies

You probably have most of the supplies and tools needed to make an Elegant Lone Star quilt; a few items may be more difficult to find.

1. Pattern Ease by HTC is a 46″-wide pattern making material sold by the yard.

2. Quilter's Gauge by Dritz (the red ruler with seam allowance holes)

3. Flat-head pins (also called flower-head pins)

4. Teflon pressing sheet

5. Water-soluble thread (wash-away basting thread)

6. Fusible web

Choose the Focus Fabric

Fabric selection is the key to successful design of an Elegant Lone Star quilt. Look for gorgeous, large-scale print fabrics. The sixteen pieces in the one-block quilt are very large. If the fabric is not stand-alone beautiful, or something you really like, you will probably not like the end result, even if you do produce a new design.

Consider fabric characteristics such as large design elements, interesting coloration, diverse values within each coloration, multiple colors, multiple motifs with variety in scale, and some resting areas.

The fabric pattern repeat is important. I prefer a 24″ repeat, which is most often found in large-scale fabric patterns. If a pattern is large scale is repeated but only every 12″, it is difficult to isolate an interesting design for this type of quilt.

12″ and 24″ repeats

In the gold fabric, each design element appears once every 24″. The plum fabric features a flower cluster that is repeated every 12″, creating no excitement in a large diamond.

Avoid fabrics that have a similar design pattern or scale repeated in an all over pattern, with little or no resting background area. I refer to this type of design as a "same old, same old" pattern. This fabric type creates a mushy looking quilt, with patterns so subtle they do not create a new, discernible design. When viewing this type of quilt, you get the feeling that you are looking at the fabric as it came off the bolt.

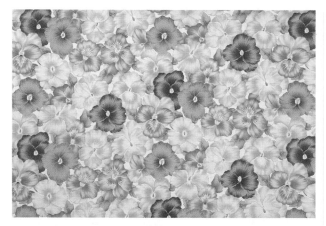

The actual design element is not as important as size, color, value, and resting areas. I have had equal success using fabrics featuring flowers, animals, fish, snakes...yes, snakes. One of my favorite Elegant Lone Star quilts is *Lora's Delight* (page 52), which had no specific motif in the fabric, but had wonderful splotches of red and purple, and nice resting areas between the splotches.

Poor choice: close repetition of design

Fair choice: The multiple design elements, colors, and resting spaces create more excitement.

Good choice: Diverse design, high-contrast coloration, adequate resting space

Where do you find these fabrics? Almost every quilt shop has a few suitable selections. When I find a fabric that appeals to me, I purchase it right away; otherwise it will not be there when I want to make a quilt. In addition to quilt shop cottons, I also occasionally select some home decorator fabrics.

Home Dec Fabrics

Decorator fabrics feature the greatest selection with large motifs. However, select only fabrics that are washable (check the end of the bolt or hanging tag on fabric on rolls) and of appropriate weight for quiltmaking (not much heavier than quilter's cotton). It can be difficult to pass up a positively beautiful home decorator fabric that does not meet the weight or washability standards for a quilt. But after dealing with the excess weight of one of these fabrics, you'll find it is a lot easier to resist the temptation. Some home decorator fabrics are very loosely woven. They ravel too much to be used in quiltmaking. Check the fabric edge for excessive fraying.

Large design elements found in home decorator fabric

Home decorator fabric used in *Floral Splendor***, page 51**

How Much Fabric to Buy

When I find a wonderful candidate for focus fabric, I purchase 6 yards. Assuming a 24″ repeat, this provides 9 repeats. Only 8 repeats are actually used, so the additional 24″ allows for some flexibility when choosing the isolated design, as you will discover in Chapter 4. If you use decorator fabric, the repeat is generally 27″, requiring 6¾ yards for 9 repeats.

Background Fabric

The squares and triangles that make up the background are also very large. A solid or tone-on-tone background provides outstanding areas for beautiful quilting motifs or for trapunto. To complement an elegant star, the supporting fabric in the background should also impart a feeling of elegance. Keep the background non competitive in scale and design so it does not overpower the central star. The background needs to remain visually in the background! In general 5 to 6 yards will be adequate, unless a large border of background fabric is used.

Good background choices

Poor background choices; fabrics are too busy

When choosing background fabric, do check different colors. If you are using a color from the focus fabric, choose a couple shades lighter or darker . This is usually much more interesting than using the exact shade.

The value of the background color will determine whether the quilt is a light-colored quilt or a dark-colored quilt. Using the lighter green background will make a much lighter quilt than using the dark green.

The background will determine the color feel of the quilt.

With the polar bear fabric, choosing a gold background will make a gold quilt, even though there is a lot of blue and white in the star. Choose the blue fabric and this will be a blue quilt.

Two choices for coordinated backgrounds

Coordinated choices

Spring Rhapsody, 94″ x 94″, machine pieced and quilted by Sue Smucker. Decorator fabric was used in the central star. Decorative machine quilting adds impact to the large background areas.

CHAPTER 4

Cut the Star Block

Explosion, 95″ × 95″, machine pieced by the author, machine quilted by Martha Creasy.

Select the Design Area

Isolation of a good design in the focus fabric is critical to a strong, elegant design within the star area. Only the area between the side angles or "elbows" (the widest part of the diamond template) and the center of the star contributes to this "new" design. In the example below, the new design is confined to the center half of the diamond.

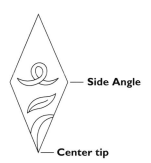

Design area of diamond

Design area of 8 identical diamonds

In fabric, multiplying a design by eight in a circle creates amazing designs. Look at the area from the side angles to the center tip. A new design emerges as eight diamonds form a star.

Design area of diamond

New design

tip   TO GAIN MORE DESIGN IMPACT, POSITION A FABRIC ELEMENT, SUCH AS AN EAGLE, IN THE CENTER OF THE DIAMOND EXTENDING OUTWARD. THIS WILL FOCUS ATTENTION ON THE LARGER AREA THAT EXPANDS THE DESIGN.

The area from the side angle to the outer tip of the diamond is totally surrounded by background fabric, so it is less important visually in establishing the new design.

Use the Template to View the Fabric

One way to isolate the design is to move the diamond template over the fabric to different potential design sites. Sometimes the fabric coloration is not strong enough to see clearly. When this happens, I use a window template or the piece of pattern making material that surrounded the cut diamond. This provides wonderful visibility of designs within the fabric.

Isolate the design with a template.

Isolate the design with a window template.

Pay special attention to four areas on the diamonds when deciding where to cut.

1. The most important area is the star center where the eight center tips of the diamonds come together.

The block requires strong central focus, so look for an interesting design element for this position. For instance, a large flower creates a wreath in the center area of the star block. Another option is to look for a design, such as, a leaf that starts near the tip, and continues further out on the diamond. This instantly provides a kaleidoscope effect.

Wreath effect (see page 92)

Kaleidoscope effect

Avoid an intense change of color or value at the inner tip, which can end up looking like a hole in the quilt. A design that is similar—but not exact—on both sides of the diamond tip would not be a good choice. When pieced, this appears to be a piecing error because the design does not exactly match on both sides of the adjacent diamonds.

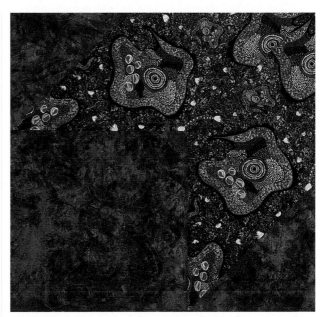

Good interest in the side angle area, from *Snakes Alive* on page 10

Poor choice for center

2. The area between the side angles (the elbows) is another opportunity for adding elements to the "new" design.

This is the largest area to be filled, so look for a design element that creates the most interest in this position. Position the large design element so that half of it is located in the center portion of the diamond, and the other half in the outer portion. This increases later design options.

3. The space about half-way between the side angles and center tip of the diamond is a third option in creating a new design. Find an area that is different in coloration or value from the side angle or tip area for this crucial position. Sometimes this will be the smallest of the design elements, and other times it will be the largest single design element from the focus fabric. When isolating this element, it is not necessary to center the design side-to-side. As the design is repeated in all eight diamonds, a wreath is created regardless of the side-to-side position of the motif within a single diamond. It is desirable however to have some resting area above and below this motif.

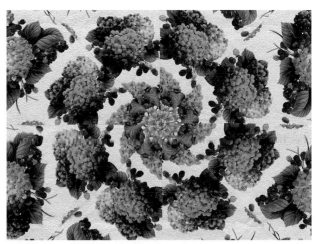

Important central area from *Spring Song* (page 60)

4. The final design area to consider is the outer tip of the diamond.

Avoid a fabric with the same color and value that you plan to use in the background. For example, using a black background fabric with a focus fabric that has a black area at the outer diamond tip will make the tip blend into the background. The diamond tips should be in high contrast to the background.

The outer tip "melts" into the background.

Look for some interest in the tips on both ends of the diamond. Remember: When the final design decisions are made, either tip may become the center of the quilt block, in spite of your original design intention.

Cut the Diamonds

1. Move the template (or the window template) over the fabric until you find the most appropriate site. Do not be concerned with grainline in this selection. The most important thing is to choose the most effective design within the focus fabric.

2. Using flat-head pins (flower-head pins), pin the diamond template to the focus fabric, positioning pins at the sides and tips. The flat-head pins allow an acrylic ruler to lie flat over the diamond template with no wobble.

Pin template to fabric.

Place the ruler on top of the template. Align the ¼″ line with the inside of the tape and its edge with the outside of the template.

3. Use your rotary cutter to cut 2 sides of the diamond.

Cut the first 2 sides.

For the other 2 sides, position the ruler on the focus fabric so it butts against the outer edge of the template. This eliminates the need to turn the fabric, so you can cut with your preferred hand. If you normally cut with both hands, position the ruler on top of the template for all 4 cuts.

tip WHEN YOU END EACH CUT, BE CAREFUL NOT TO CUT INTO THE ADJOINING AREA. YOU MIGHT WANT TO USE THE SAME AREA FOR SMALLER EIGHT-POINTED STAR BLOCKS (SEE PAGE 73).

Alternate method for cutting 2 sides

4. Unpin the template from the first diamond. Insert a pin in the diamond's center. This will mark your guide diamond, which is used to cut each new one. If you always use the same diamond as the guide, even if it is off by a whisker there will be no harm done. Avoid using each new diamond to cut the next one, or a slight variation will be multiplied 8 times, and that whisker becomes a whole beard of difference between Diamond 1 and Diamond 8.

5. Move the first diamond over the focus fabric until you find the identical design. Carefully align the diamond with the design lines in the fabric.

6. Place the diamond template on top of the guide diamond. Pin the 3 layers together at the sides, then at the tips. This pins the template, the guide diamond, and the uncut focus fabric together.

7. Place the ruler on the template, as described in Step 1. If the template ever gets sliced off a bit, the inside edge of the tape will be intact, providing the accuracy needed. (Yes, this occasionally happens—these are very long cuts!)

8. Continue the cutting process until you have cut all 8 diamonds. Be sure to use the guide diamond (the first one cut) to locate each new diamond. Always pin the template to the top for more accurate cutting.

Design With the Diamonds

It's time to get to the exciting part! Place all eight diamonds on your design wall, or on the floor, with the selected design area toward the center of the block. Stand back 6′ or more from your design. Are you pleased with the result? Do you see new elements creating some excitement that you had not even considered in the original selection process?

This is the first option available for the quilt.

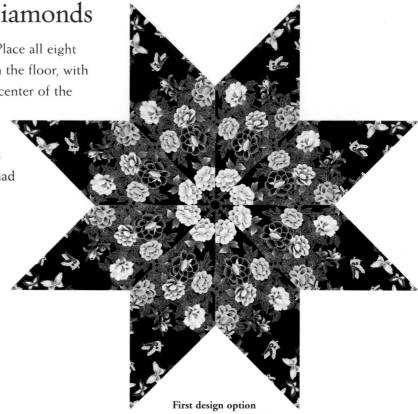

First design option

For a second design option, turn each of the eight diamonds around, so the center tip becomes the outer tip. Again, step back 6′ or more. How do you like the second design option? About 50 percent of the time, the second design is better than the first.

From the two options, I chose the second to use for my quilt. Which option would you choose?

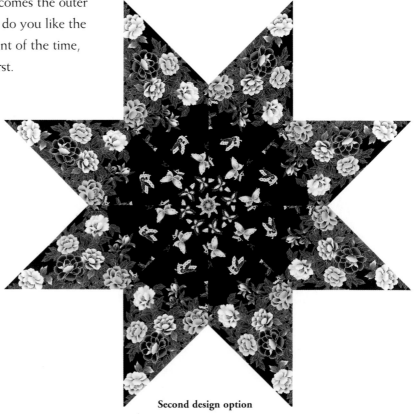

Second design option

Cut the Squares

Star Blocks 65″ or Less

Squares are cut from the background fabric. If your star block is 65″ or less, you can cut all 4 squares at once.

1. Fold the fabric as it came off the bolt, then bring both ends together. This creates 4 layers of fabric. Using flat-head pins, pin the square template to the background fabric. Place a pin at each corner.

2. Cover the edge of the template with the ruler, aligning the ¼″ marking on the ruler with the inside of the tape, and the edge with the outside of the template. Cut the 4 squares.

Cut 4 squares.

3. If necessary, place the ruler on the fabric and butt it next to the taped template to cut with your hand of preference.

Star Blocks Larger than 70″

The fabric is not wide enough to yield 4 squares across. For these larger-size blocks, unfold the fabric and bring the cut ends together to make 2 layers. Cut 2 squares, reposition the template, and cut the remaining 2 squares.

Cut the Triangles

Four triangles are needed for the background. It is very important to cut the triangles with the longest edge on the straight of grain. These can all be cut at once.

1. With the background fabric folded in 4 layers, as you did when cutting the 65″ or smaller squares, position the long side of the triangle template parallel with the selvage.

2. Pin at each corner with flat-head pins.

3. Place the ruler on the template, aligning the ¼″ line with the inside of the tape and the edge with the outside of the template. Cut 4 triangles.

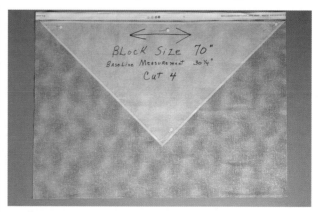

Cut 4 triangles.

Elegant Japanese Star, 82″ x 95″,
machine pieced by Maxine Holmes,
machine quilted by Vickie Yanik. This
two-color quilt shows off several wreaths
in both very light and very dark values.
Subtle secondary designs appear within
the dark areas. Beautiful feather quilting
complements the open background
spaces.

Piece the Star Block

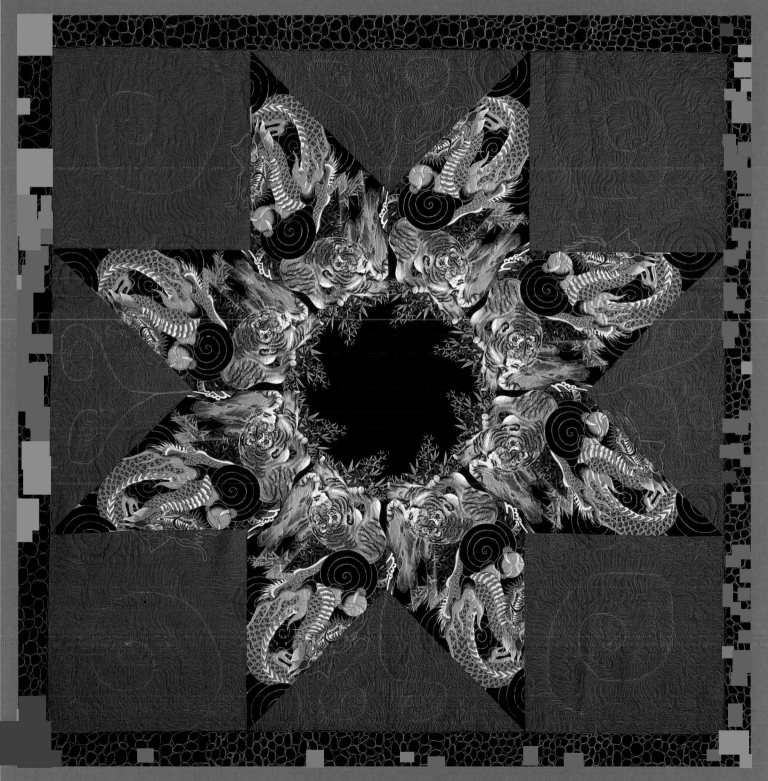

On the Prowl, 85″ × 85″, machine pieced and quilted by the author.

Jessica's Dream, 60″ x 96″, machine pieced and quilted by Becky Thomas. Many pieced stars dance around the center star. The focus fabric creates an interesting combination of wreaths and stars. Additional borders substantially lengthen the quilt for a twin-size bed.

An eight-pointed star has always been the block quilters "love to hate." They love the block, but don't enjoy piecing all the set-in seams. Many years ago, Sharyn Craig showed me a method for piecing an eight-pointed star block without set-in seams. A variation of this method works well for piecing this oversized eight-pointed star block.

The block is pieced from the outside toward the center, a method I refer to as "backward piecing." The benefits of this method are accurate outer star points, a perfectly pieced center, and side angles (elbows) without puckers or pleats.

Prepare for Sewing

Before taking that first stitch, prepare your sewing machine for an accurate ¼″ seam allowance. In drafting this block, we added a ¼″ seam allowance; now it is important to know exactly how to "stitch off" that exact amount. The block consists of three different shapes: diamond, triangle, and square. To make these parts fit together, a ¼″ seam allowance must be maintained from the beginning to the end of every stitching line. The following "Helpers" make seamline accuracy simpler.

HELPER 1: Add a ¼″ Tape Guide

Many machines have a ¼″ piecing foot. This foot allows ¼″ from the center of the needle to the edge of the presser foot. However, it does not tell you where to line up the fabrics to maintain the ¼″ seam allowance in front of the needle. Even if a ¼″ foot is used, it is important to establish a ¼″ line in front of the foot so these long seams can be lined up correctly prior to feeding them under the presser foot.

1. Position a ruler with very thin lines under the foot, so the ¼″ line is under the center of the needle. Carefully lower the needle until it touches the ¼″ mark on the ruler. (I use a Dritz Quilter's Gauge 6″ red ruler, which has holes at various increments, including ¼″ from the edge. The needle can be lowered through this ruler.) Gently lower the presser foot to hold the ruler in place.

2. Move the ruler until it is parallel with a straight vertical line on the sewing machine, such as the edge of the throat plate, or a long marking on the throat plate.

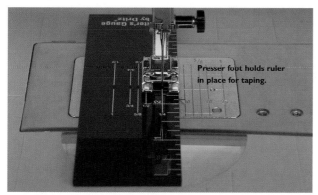

Establish ¼″ seam allowance using a ruler.

3. Insert the tip of your utility scissors into a roll of masking tape, several layers from the outside of the tape. I prefer painter's masking tape because it leaves no residue on the throat plate. It can be found in primary colors at any paint store. Cut through several layers of the tape.

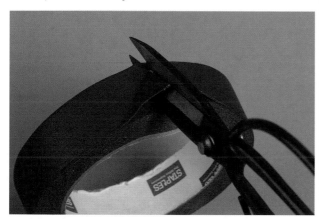

Cut several layers of tape.

4. Remove a 4″-long section of tape and place the tape next to the ruler. The tape should touch the ruler edge and can extend back past the presser foot if there are no feed dogs exposed outside the presser foot. If partial areas of the feed dogs are exposed, cut the tape at the front edge of the presser foot.

> **tip** DO NOT COVER ANY PORTION OF THE FEED DOGS WITH TAPE. ALSO, DO NOT APPLY ANY TAPE UNDER THE PRESSER FOOT, WHERE IT CONTACTS THE THROAT PLATE. YOUR MACHINE WILL NOT FUNCTION PROPERLY IF EITHER HAPPENS.

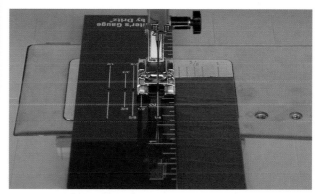

Butt the tape flush against the ruler.

Note: If you use the needle position to establish ¼″ seams, apply the tape after establishing ¼″ according to the method outlined above.

HELPER 2: Tape Guide for the Diamond Angle

It helps to make a tape guide that identifies where to position the pin and end the line of stitching.

1. On the back of the diamond template, place ¼″ masking tape on the seam allowance for about 1½″ in both directions from the side angle.

2. Trim the tape at the outer edge of the template shape. I refer to this as Tape Guide 135°, since that is the angle's measure.

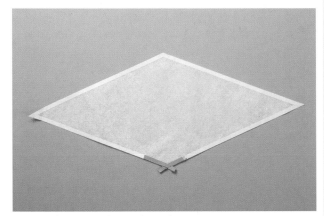

Tape Guide 135° on diamond template

HELPER 3: Tape Guide for Triangle and Square

1. Use ¼˝ masking tape to tape the corner of the triangle template in the same way.

2. Trim the outer edges. I refer to this as Tape Guide 90°, since that is the angle. It is used on both triangle and square background fabric pieces.

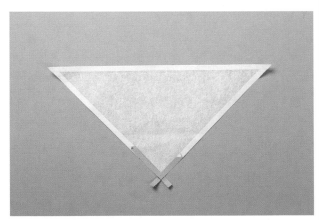

Tape Guide 90°

3. Remove the 135° and 90° Tape Guides from the templates. Stick them to the front of your sewing machine for easy access during construction.

Stitch the Lone Star Block

These instructions are for stitching a quarter of the total quilt block. To make the entire block, repeat these steps 4 times.

1. Place the diamonds in 2 stacks, 4 in each stack. Position all of the diamonds with the design area you chose for the center closest to you.

2. Place a stack of triangles between the 2 diamond stacks. These 3 stacks are pieced into units. I refer to them as "kite" units because of their shape.

Layout for piecing units

3. Pick up a diamond and a triangle from the stack on the right and with the diamond on top of the triangle, align the pointed tips. Place a pin approximately 1˝ to the left of the edge to be seamed. The pin will be parallel to the seamline, but far enough from the edge to permit stitching without removing the pin. This keeps the layers from shifting when you stitch.

4. Insert the next pin at the side angle of the diamond. The pieces are slightly different angles at this point. Even experienced quilters have difficulty finding the perfect "spot" for this pin. Using Tape Guide 135° on the diamond and Tape Guide 90° on the square removes all the guesswork about where to pin and stitch. Simply place the pin at the inside intersection of the 2 pieces of tape.

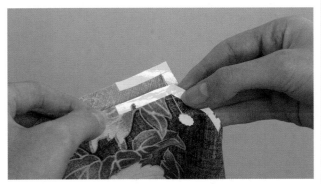

Correct pin placement in diamond and triangle

5. Pin the side angle area by inserting a pin through the inside intersections of the tape guides on the diamond and triangle. Bring the layers snugly together and pin. Insert another pin to hold both long seam edges together in this position.

6. Remove the tape guides before you pin the remainder of the seamline. Add more pins between the pins at each end. It might look like 1 fabric piece is longer than the other. To get them into pinning position, hold both previously pinned areas, one in each hand, and "fluff" the 2 pieces gently up and down on the tabletop. Using the back of your fingernails, "scratch" the fabric with a backward motion to align the two edges. These edges are bias; this positioning technique eliminates undue stretching of edges. I call this the "fluff and scratch" technique.

7. Once the edges are aligned, pin 1″ from the edge, parallel to the edge of the fabric.

8. Lower the machine needle all the way down. With the diamond on top, align the outer point of the pinned unit with the ¼″ tape guide. Slide the fabrics back toward the needle. When the fabric unit touches the needle, lower the presser foot and begin stitching.

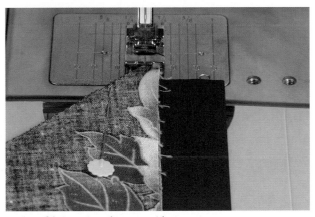

Position fabric against the tape guide.

Keeping the fabric straight against the tape, and using the needle-down position to determine exactly where to begin stitching, will ensure a perfect ¼″ seam at the outer edge of the block. Points will not be cut off, or floating, when the first border is added to the block.

9. Stitch from the outer point to the opposite end. From the right side, gently press the seam toward the diamond.

Stitched Diamond/Triangle unit

10. Pick up a diamond from the stack on the left. Place the sewn unit on top of the diamond. The background triangle point will line up perfectly with the point of the diamond. Pin 1″ from the edge, parallel to the stitching edge.

11. Use the tape guides for pin placement at the side-angle area. Insert a pin through the inside intersections of the tape guides on the diamond and the triangle. Bring the layers snugly together and pin. With a second pin, secure the 2 layers in position. Use the "fluff and scratch" method to align the 2 long edges together, pinning 1″ from the outer edge.

Pin the diamond/triangle unit to the diamond.

12. Lower the needle and place the pieces next to the tape on your machine. Slide the layers toward the needle. Stitch from the outside point, stopping just as you reach the previous seamline. Do not stitch into or beyond the previous seamline. Backtack aggressively (at least 5 stitches)!

Stop stitching before crossing the previous seamline.

13. From the right side, gently press the seam toward the diamond.

14. Lay out the stitched unit. Double-check the design area created by the diamonds. Are they positioned so the same design motif will meet at the center diamond tips? If so, the diamonds can be stitched together to finish the unit. With the second diamond on top, pin the diamond tips together, aligning them perfectly. Apply the tape guide to the diamond at the angle. The bottom diamond does not need to be taped. Place a pin at the tape intersection, then through the end of the previous stitching line on the bottom diamond. Snug the 2 diamonds together, adding another pin.

15. Keeping the second diamond on top, pin 1″ from the edges, as previously described, fluffing and scratching the fabrics into position. Place the diamonds next to the tape guide and slide them back toward the lowered needle. Stitch from the tips of the diamonds toward the triangle.

Pin and stitch the 2 diamonds together.

16. Do not stitch into the previous seams. Stop at the edge of the pin in the intersection. Backtack aggressively.

17. Press the seam in a clockwise direction. To do this, place the unit right side up, with the background to the left, and press gently away from you.

18. Place the pieced unit on top of a square. Trim the "dog ears" (the tips of the diamond seam allowances) that extend beyond the square. Do not trim the seams at the center diamond points.

19. Pin the edges. Use tape guides on both the diamond and the square. Pinning at the tape intersections will line up the edges perfectly. "Fluff and scratch" the fabrics into position. Stitch from the outer edge toward the center.

Finished unit with square attached

Reminder: This unit represents a quarter of the total quilt block. Repeat the above steps to make 3 additional quarters.

Join Two Quarters of the Star Block

1. Place 2 units together with a square on top of the outer edge of a diamond. Use Tape Guide 135° on the right side of the diamond, and Tape Guide 90° on the wrong side of the square/diamond unit. Pin snugly at the tape intersections. Align the edges of the units, pinning 1˝ from the edge to be sewn. Pin the entire seam, after fluffing and scratching into place.

2. Stitch from the outside edge to the previous seam at the angle. Do not stitch into the previous stitching line; this will create a pucker. Backtack aggressively. From the front, press the seam toward the diamond.

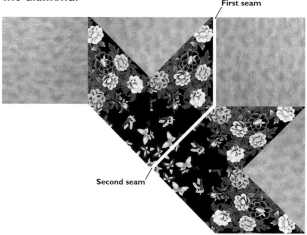

Two completed units

3. Join the center half of the diamonds. At the tips in the center, previously sewn seams will nest together. Keep them tight together with the tips

aligned. Pin in place. At the side angle, pin through the end of the stitching on the top diamond, and through the Tape Guide 135° intersection on the bottom diamond. Place the remaining pins about 1˝ from the edge. Stitch from the tips outward, stopping at the previous seam. Do not stitch into the previous seam to avoid puckering. Press the seam in a clockwise direction. Repeat for the remaining 2 quarters of the star block.

Sew the Block Halves Together

1. Place the quilt halves right side up. Sew the squares to the diamonds. Place one of the squares over the adjacent diamond on the other half. Be careful to line up the correct side of the square. Follow the same taping, pinning, and alignment directions as in joining quarters.

2. Stitch from the outside edge to the side angle of the diamonds. Repeat with the other side of the quilt.

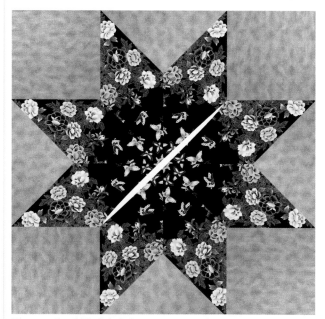

Two completed block halves

3. The last seam crosses the center of the block. Before pinning, trim the "dog ears." To reduce bulk in the center, trim the seams that joined the quarters. Trim only one side of each seam to ⅛". Leaving one side of the seam intact protects the strength of this previous seam.

Center prior to grading

Graded seam

4. Pin the center seam together, beginning at the center. Place a pin directly through the spot where all the diamond seams meet. Before pinning to the other layer check on the right side to be sure the pin is in the proper position. Begin stitching at one side angle, backtack, then stitch to the center. Slow down as you approach the center. This area contains more layers of fabric because multiple seams meet in the center of the quilt. This thickness will encourage the layers to ease back from the ¼" marking.

Sew slowly so you can control the fabric placement while stitching. Sew the remainder of the seam, backtacking at the end.

5. Press the final seam open to distribute the center bulk. Finger-press open, then use an iron. Turn the quilt to the right side and press the center seam again, checking for accuracy.

tip AN ALTERNATE WAY TO APPROACH THE CENTER SEAM IS TO MACHINE BASTE 4" OR 5" THROUGH THE CENTER. IF THE CENTER LOOKS GOOD, CHANGE TO A NORMAL STITCH LENGTH, THEN STITCH THE ENTIRE SEAM.

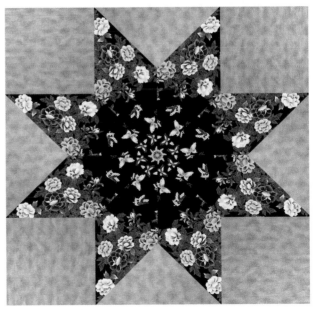

Completed 70" block

Pressing Tips

Many pieces in these quilts have long bias edges. It is very easy to stretch these edges when pressing.

1. Press all seams, except for the center seam of the eight-pointed star, from the right side of the fabric.

2. Place the piece on your ironing board, with the seam in the direction to be pressed facing away from you. The fabric in front of the seam should lie flat on the board. The fabric over the seam should round up higher than the board.

Fabric placement for pressing

3. Use the side of the iron—not the tip—for all pressing. Using the tip of the iron will stretch the fabric. Set the iron on the front fabric (closest to you) and press back over the seam. Do not set any part of the iron on top of the seam to begin pressing to avoid making a small pleat at the seamline. When the iron is directly over the seam, stop moving the iron to permit heat from the iron to flatten the seam.

Lift the iron and move it over to the next area to be ironed. Repeat until the seam is complete. Be very cautious to use as little iron movement as possible. This is not "ironing," just "pressing."

Press with the side of the iron.

4. The center seam of an eight-pointed star should be pressed open to distribute excess bulk. Working from the wrong side of the block, spread the seam allowances with your fingers; tilt the iron so only the side of it sits right on top of the stitched center.

Tilt the iron to open the seam.

5. Heat from the iron will help to open the seam, which in the center area includes multiple seams joined at the center. When the seam is opened, set the iron flat on the seam. Continue pressing from the center outward; repeat for the other half of the center seam. Turn the block over and press it flat on the right side.

6

Enhance the Background

Hydrangea Stars, 85″ × 85″, machine pieced by Sheryl Hardesty, machine quilted by Martha Creasy. The periwinkle colorway of the fabric used in ***Spring Song*** (page 60) creates a warm central star. The outer stars circle the focus star in an unusual set.

Divide Background Areas

Background pieces for an Elegant Lone Star are extremely large. Their size provides many opportunities to enhance the central block. Some effective options follow.

1. Large wreaths or other fanciful types of quilting look beautiful in the larger design areas. In *Inspiration* (page 6) the background areas showcase the quilting.

Background areas provide space for fancy quilting.

2. Trapunto by machine is a very easy way to add an extra "Wow" factor in background areas. As viewers look at your quilt, they spontaneously say, "wow!" The background areas of *Twist and Turn* (page 56) feature trapunto in the feather designs.

Trapunto adds an exquisite touch.

3. Try inserting smaller 8-pointed stars centered within the background areas. The small stars in *Twin Number I* (page 8) twinkle in the print background.

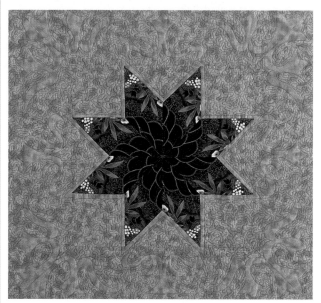

Stars centered in background areas

4. Insert 8-pointed star blocks at the outer edge of the main block to create a border of star blocks. The small blocks in *Fantasia Night Star* (page 79) form a border within the borders.

Stars form a border.

5. Use Broderie Perse appliqué to echo the inner design elements; appliqué by hand or machine. The wonderful flowers in *Spring Song* (page 60) were perfect for applique.

Variations on a Star, 98" x 98", machine pieced and hand quilted by Joann Wackenheim. The Asian fabric provided some resting areas to emphasize the various flower wreaths. Small outer stars frame the intricate hand quilting.

6. Reverse appliqué is a faster version of using focus fabric design elements. Cut a window into the background, which provides a view to select the best design. Circles reveal the flowers in *Happiness…Is Color* (page 92).

Reverse appliqué

7. Background pieces can be divided by inserting a new pattern. In *Ivory Stampede* (page 82), the background squares were divided by the pieced spiky points used in the border.

Background broken up by spiky points

The ways to enhance these large backgrounds are infinite, limited only by our imagination.

Swirley Jo Bob, 85″ x 85″, machine pieced and quilted by Wendy Lewis. Curved outer star points and the twisting border gives a happy contemporary feeling. Color changes in the background keep the eye moving around the quilt.

CHAPTER 7

Borders

African Tribute, 78″ × 95″, machine pieced by the author, machine quilted by Vickie Yanik. A different border on each side of the quilt reflects styles found in African art quilts.

Border Options

Borders can be used simply to frame the quilt, or to continue the design action. A simple frame for the "big block" is a quick and easy way to complete a project. A frame can be any number of borders or fabrics. Leftover star fabric can be used as one of the borders to provide a sense of unity with the center.

I recommend using straight-of-grain cuts for all borders. Even if I have to piece the borders for length, I cut the border strips on the lengthwise grain (parallel to the selvages). Although crosswise grain borders require smaller yardage amounts, they tend to stretch. Likewise, mixing some lengthwise grain and crosswise grain strips will usually result in some wavy and distorted areas in the border. When I do use crosswise grain strips, it is only for tiny accent borders, and I make sure that I do not stretch them while sewing.

I prefer mitering the corners of my borders, especially when I use several different borders. Instead of sewing each different border piece to the quilt, I sew them together, first aligning the center of each piece, and then add them in one trip around the quilt.

Springtime Flowers, 92" x 92", machine pieced by the author, quilted by Carol Hardesty.
The border serves as a frame for the inner design.

Floater Borders Visually Protect Star Tips

Sometimes all you need is a "floater border." This is a border of the same fabric as the background fabric. Floater borders protect the visual sharpness of the outer points. When a border is added to the big block, if it is a different color than the background, being off by even the width of one fabric thread will show at the outer tips. Adding any width of floater border eliminates this frustration. I usually add a 1″ to 3″ floater border. *Floral Splendor* features only a floater border and the binding serves as a frame for the quilt.

Floral Splendor, 85″ x 85″, pieced by the author, hand quilted by Marjorie Gunn. The floater border visually protects the star tips.

Use Leftover Focus Fabric to Piece Borders

The fabric left after cutting the diamonds can be utilized for smaller, new design eight-pointed star blocks. Using these small stars for borders brings the focus fabric out into the border area and continues the design action.

Stars can be pieced as whole or half stars for the straight edges of borders, or as three-quarter stars to go around a corner. See page 74 for directions to cut and piece these smaller stars from leftover focus fabric.

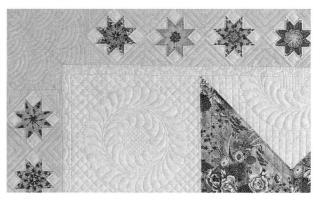

Small stars set on point from *Variations on a Star* (page 47)

This portion of *Angie's Star* (page 73)was elongated by adding larger blocks on the top and bottom.

Consider Focus Fabric for Traditional Borders

Traditional pieced borders, such as the checkerboard squares in *Lora's Delight*, or braided borders as in *African Tribute* (page 49), also contribute to visual interest.

Lora's Delight, 82″ x 82″, pieced by the author, quilted by Vickie Yanik. An interesting border treatment: a checkerboard made from the focus fabric.

Appliqué Borders Add Interest

Both traditional and Broderie Perse appliqué can be used, separately or together, to create an outstanding border effect. The border in *Spring Song* (page 60) uses a companion fabric for a traditional appliqué swag, combined with elements cut from the focus fabric used for Broderie Perse. A machine appliqué stitch pattern was coupled with 40-weight rayon variegated thread to add a little extra pizzazz to the machine appliqué.

Some quilters plan every aspect of the quilt. I rarely plan more than the central block. After piecing, I put the block on my design wall for further study and development.

When I plan the total quilt, quite often I find that the border treatment in my mind's eye is not nearly as effective on the quilt as I thought it would be. An example of this is *Blue Rhapsody*, for which I stitched small eight-pointed star blocks out of the focus fabric. When added to the quilt, they looked wimpy. Because of the very dark fabric used to convert the Elegant Lone Star to a giant feathered star, the lighter blue and white blocks appeared to be something added on to make the quilt larger, rather than an important design aspect. Switching to the same dark blue used in the feathers provided a wonderful border with a very strong, graphic effect.

Blocks from focus fabric

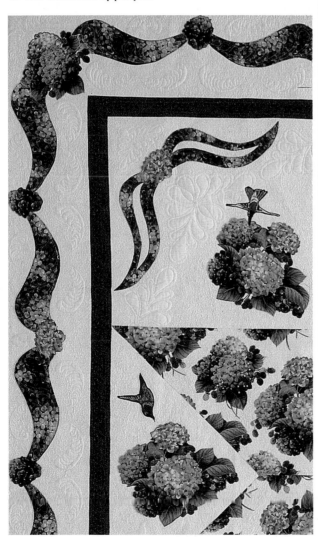

A combination of traditional and Broderie Perse appliqué

Blue Rhapsody, 100″ x 100″, machine pieced by
the author, machine quilted by Vickie Yanik. This
quilt features a graphic outer star border

Final Border Decisions

My advice is to wait on the final border decisions until the star block is complete. As you audition fabrics, or various pieced and appliquéd units, let your visual instinct have a big voice in the decision. As I add fabrics, or pieced units, to the design wall for consideration, I step back 6′ or more to test my reaction. When looking at the addition, if I get a hard knot in my stomach, I know this is a terrible choice. If I feel warm and fuzzy, I know this will be a super choice for the border. If I get no feeling— good or bad—I consider the choice to be just okay. It will probably not ruin the overall effect, but it will not make it great either.

King Kamahaha Day, 60″ x 60″, machine pieced and quilted by Wendy Lewis. Contrast of colors glows within the star. Focus fabric elements used in Broderie Perse and in the undulating border.

Trapunto

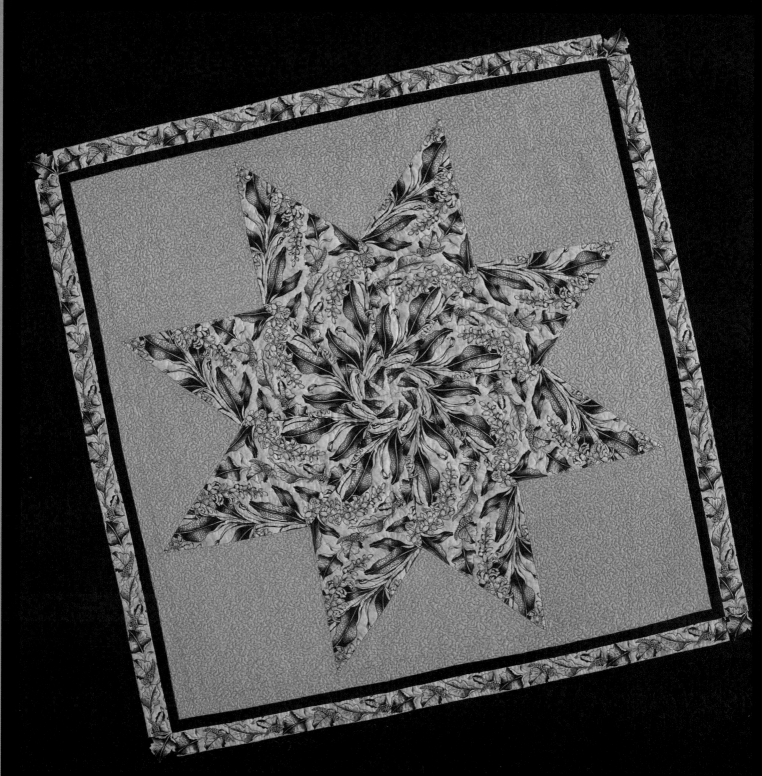

Twist and Turn, 84″ × 84″, machine pieced by the author, machine quilted by Gail Miller.

Trapunto Adds Depth to Quilting

Machine trapunto is a quick and easy technique that adds dimension and depth to areas within the quilt. Prior to quilting, add an extra layer of batting to drawn designs to produce puffiness in that area. Use a water-soluble basting thread to attach the extra layer of batting. The thread washes out after the quilting is complete. Trapunto is usually done in background areas within the block or in the borders. The step-by-step instructions that follow produce incredible results.

1. *Establish Orientation Lines:* To center the design, establish fold lines by folding the fabric in half, both horizontally and vertically.

Press the folds. Fold the fabric diagonally to establish diagonal fold lines. Press folds.

2. *Select and Transfer the Design:* Use quilting stencils with closed designs. These stencils are held together with little bridges. To use, place a quilting stencil on top of the fabric to transfer the design. After tracing, there will be spaces in the design, left by skipping the bridges. Connect all design lines because a solid line will be needed when machine stitching.

Some wonderful designs can be found on paper patterns. To use a paper pattern, place the fabric over the design and trace the design, using a source of light under the paper pattern.

New patterns can also be created by hand drawing or copying elements found in fabric, coloring books, and so on. I use Pattern Ease to draw this type of pattern. It can then be pinned under the fabric, and using a lightbox or window, the pattern is easily traced onto fabric.

Drawn design

Transfer the entire design, including trapunto lines and interior quilting lines. The line must be very visible, but removable. For light fabrics, I use a blue chemical marking pencil. (Pretest any marking tool to be sure the lines can be removed, and do not press the lines—they could become permanent.) Chalk marking products work well for dark fabrics.

Transfer the design to the fabric

3. *Attach Stuffing:* Pin a piece of polyester batting large enough to cover the design to the wrong side of the fabric.

Pin batting to the wrong side of the fabric.

This is the "stuffing" batting. If the stuffed area is small, you may need a thicker type of batting to produce the desired dimension. In large trapunto areas, such as feather wreaths, a polyester batting with a fleece-like feel works well. Polyester batting is the best choice since it retains its loft. Polyester battings with a "cotton candy" density are not good choices.

4. *Prepare Machine for Stitching:* Thread your machine with water-soluble (wash-away) basting thread. Use this thread in both the top and bobbin.
Using this thread in both positions eliminates the possibility of the bobbin thread poking though to the top of the quilt after the top thread is washed away. Lower the feed dogs, if this option is available on your machine, and use a darning foot. This puts your machine in "free-motion mode." Free motion means the fabric, with the batting attached, can be moved freely under the darning foot for machine stitching. The "stuffing" batting is attached to the fabric in a free-motion procedure.

5. *Stitch Trapunto Batting in Place:* Bring the bobbin thread up to the top—hold the top thread while taking a single stitch, then pull the bobbin thread to the top of the fabric. Stitch around the exterior of the design. Do NOT stitch the interior quilting lines marked within the design. Don't worry if you get a little off the line. When immersed in water, this stitching line disappears. This is wonderful practice for free-motion machine quilting.

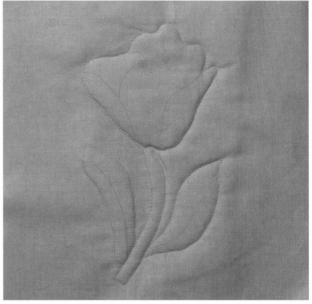

Stitch on the marked exterior line.

✴ *tip* AS SOON AS THE STITCHING IS COMPLETE, REMOVE THE BOBBIN AND SPOOL OF WATER-SOLUBLE THREAD AND STORE THEM IN A SEALED PLASTIC BAG. THIS THREAD IS AFFECTED BY HUMIDITY, SO SEALING OUT THE AIR IS IMPORTANT FOR LONGEVITY. INSTANT REMOVAL FROM THE MACHINE ENSURES THAT THE THREAD WILL NOT BE MISTAKENLY USED AS STITCHING THREAD. IMAGINE THE DISASTER OF STITCHING A GARMENT WITH THIS THREAD, THEN BEING CAUGHT IN A RAINSTORM!

6. *Clip Excess Batting:* Clip batting ¹⁄₁₆″ from the stitching. It is very easy to clip into the fabric doing this step. To avoid this, turn the unit over so the batting is on top and the fabric on the bottom. Position your index finger under the line to be clipped. As the scissors trim the excess batting, the "under finger" will feel if the fabric is about to be clipped. Keep moving your finger position under the stitched line as you continue to clip.

Once the fabric and batting are joined and the excess batting is trimmed, I treat this as one layer.

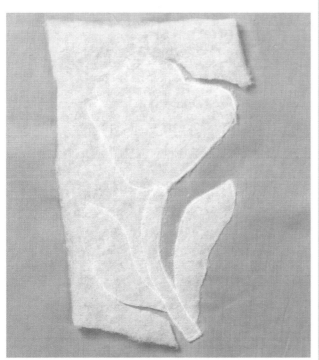

Batting partially clipped

7. *Construction With Trapunto:* If you added the trapunto to individual blocks, they are now ready to be assembled into a quilt top. Trapunto can also be added after the top of the quilt is pieced together, prior to layering for quilting.

8. Quilting With Trapunto: When you are ready to quilt, layer the backing, batting, and quilt top with the trapunto batting already attached and clipped away. Pin closely to the trapunto areas to prevent the stuffing from pulling fabric out of straight of grain. After doing the stabilizing quilting (see page 61), quilt the trapunto areas. Quilt right over the previous stitching—the wash-away stitching will disappear when the quilt is immersed in cool water, leaving only the actual quilting. Quilt the interior markings on the trapunto designs.

Detail of quilted trapunto from *Elegant Japanese Star* (page 34)

CHAPTER 9

Finish Your Quilt

Spring Song, 89″ × 89″, machine pieced and quilted by the author. Broderie Perse and swag appliques, free-motion thread-painted birds and beading of the flower petals and inside edge of the binding add delightful surprises to this quilt.

Quilting

Either hand or machine quilting is appropriate for an Elegant Lone Star quilt. Background areas present large open spaces for beautiful quilting designs. Be sure to maintain balance in the amount of quilting to help ensure that the quilt will lie flat or hang straight. Different types of quilting, such as straight lines, curvy designs, stippling, and crosshatching, add interest. To further enhance the quilting effect, try using trapunto (see Chapter 8).

Stabilize Quilting

Stabilize your quilt before adding design quilting. Quilting in-the-ditch on the outside of the central star stabilizes this large area. For in-the-ditch quilting, stitch right beside the seams instead of exactly over the stitching line. (Piercing previous piecing stitches with quilting could weaken or even cut the piecing thread.) Monofilament (invisible) thread is a good choice for this quilting, with a cotton thread that matches the backing in the bobbin. Ditch stitching between some or all of the borders helps to keep them straight, stabilizing this large exterior area. Stitch on the "low side" of the seam. The high side includes the top fabric and two layers of seam allowance fabric; stitching on the high side creates an unsightly ridge.

Embellishments for the Star

Large design elements in the focus fabric offer a premarked pattern, which reduces the time required for marking a quilting design. After quilting around and within a design element, such as a flower cluster, travel to the next design by a combination of curvy lines and circles, or by a meander type of quilting. The print in *Spring Song* served as the quilting design.

Quilting the fabric design lines

Quilt the Trapunto Areas

All areas of trapunto should be outlined with quilting. Quilt right over the previous water-soluble thread line of stitching. The wash-away thread around the feathers will disappear when the quilt is immersed in water.

Quilted trapunto design from *Twist and Turn* (page 56)

Quilt the lines marked within the trapunto design. Stipple quilting (very close quilting) around the trapunto will make the stuffed area appear more dimensional.

Faux Trapunto

You can also achieve the look of trapunto without adding a "stuffing batting" (see page 58). This is called Faux Trapunto. Use a wool batting, which retains loft; quilt the design, then stipple very closely next to the design. As I machine quilt, I pretend I am driving bumper cars at the carnival—I keep bumping the design outline with stitching as stippling is added. This prevents a ridge from forming between the quilting and the design. Close stippling will compress the quilt sandwich, making the designs appear to be stuffed. This is a real time-saver, as no advance stitching of the design and batting, or clipping away is required.

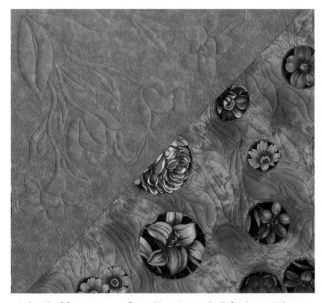

A detail of faux trapunto from *Happiness…Is Color* (page 92)

Faux Appliqué

Often, an error in quiltmaking becomes something more wonderful than we could have imagined. This happened to me in *Surprise*. I had selected an elegant dark eggplant background, a color I truly loved. After piecing the quilt, I hated the color. It was so intense in the large background areas that all I saw was the background. To shift visual emphasis to the star, I selected a light blue thread for small meander quilting in the eggplant background. I then placed a stencil design in each background area, which I left totally unquilted. Imagine my surprise when the quilt was finished, and the stencil design areas appeared to be appliquéd—thus the name faux appliqué! The light blue thread totally changed the intensity of the background areas, letting the star dominate the quilt.

Quilting creates faux appliqué.

Border Treatments

Borders can be "free-form" quilted or quilted with a marked pattern. They can be treated as individual elements, with the design contained within each border, or they can be combined by using a pattern that covers two or more borders with one design. This type of quilting eliminates the need to stitch in-the-ditch between borders.

Quilting multiple borders with one design, a portion of *Flower Power* (page 84)

Surprise, 78″ x 78″, pieced by the author, quilted by Vickie Yanik. Faux appliqué is an interesting embellishment.

Exquisite Delight, 88″ x 102″, machine pieced and hand quilted by Bernice Shoeppner. A pillow tuck, crosshatched with hand quilting, was added above the central star to lengthen the quilt. Pieced stars lie on top of the pillows, echoing the central star. The large background areas are elaborately hand quilted.

Trim the Quilt

Trim the edges of the quilt, if necessary, to establish straight lines and square corners. Use a walking foot and stitch the quilt layers (top, backing, and batting) together ⅛″ from the edge of the quilt. Applying the binding is so much easier if the quilt edges are already secured.

Binding

The first time I entered a quilt in a judged show was a real wake-up call to problems in this last step of making a quilt. My binding had either curved or pointed corners and was not filled with batting to the edge, all the finishing stitches that should have been invisible were showing, and the binding was not straight on the edges of the quilt. After lots of trial and error, I have found many steps that will guarantee good, secure bindings. For straight quilt edges, I prefer crossgrain binding because it is easier to apply without stretching the quilt edges. Bindings must be cut on bias for quilts with curves or points in the quilt edges.

Cut Binding Strips

Cut binding strips 2″ wide on the crossgrain. Add the length of all four sides of the quilt and add 12″ to determine the total length of the binding. Divide by 40″ (or the width of your fabric) to determine the number of strips needed. For example, if your quilt measures 95″ × 95″, you will need a total of 392″ of binding, or 10 strips.

tip FOR FASTER CUTTING, PLACE A RULER AT THE 6″ MARK AND CUT. WITHOUT LIFTING THE RULER, SLIDE IT TO 4″ AND CUT. SLIDE THE RULER TO 2″ AND CUT. YOU NOW HAVE 3 STRIPS READY TO STACK. REPEAT UNTIL YOU HAVE THE CORRECT NUMBER OF STRIPS.

Cut the Angles

1. Place all the strips on top of each other, RIGHT SIDE UP. With the ruler's 45° line on the long edge of the stacked strips, cut the ends at an angle.

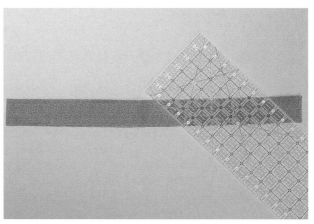

Cut at a 45° angle.

2. Keep the strips right side up and turn the stack around so the angled cuts are on your right. Place the ruler in the same position as for the previous cut.

3. Cut the ends at a 45° angle. The angle might look wrong, but it will be just right for joining to the other end of the strips.

Join Strips to Make a Continuous Binding

1. Sew the strips in pairs, letting the tips of the seam allowance extend on each side. Lower the machine needle and slide the pieces toward the needle until the intersection of the strips touches the needle. Stitch to the intersection on the opposite side. It will not matter if this is a perfect ¼″, as long as the width is consistent.

Join strips.

2. Stitch all strips together to make one continuous binding. Press all the seams open to distribute bulk in the binding. Press the binding strip in half horizontally.

Attach the Binding to the Quilt

1. Place the end of the binding on the edge of the quilt, near the center of one side. Arrange the binding around the edge of the quilt. If a binding seam lands at any of the four corners, adjust the beginning position to avoid this. The extra bulk from the seam would make it impossible to fold in a nice corner.

2. Lengthen your stitch length to a basting length, 3.5 to 4.0. Leaving about 8″ of the binding free, begin to stitch the binding to the layers. Stitch for about 10″, using a ¼″ seam allowance. Remove the quilt from the machine and roll the folded edge of the binding to the back. Different weights of batting

and fabrics can cause the ¼″ seam allowance to be an inappropriate width. Check to see if the binding width is the same width on the front and the back of the quilt; also check to see if the binding covers the machine stitching. Make any adjustments, then change the stitch length to 2.5 and sew the binding to the layers.

3. Stop about 4″ before the corner. With the binding held at the corner of the quilt, fold it back at a 45° angle.

Angle for folding binding

4. Crease this folded angle in the binding. Place the binding back on the edge of the quilt. You will be able to see the crease line in the binding. Put a pin over the crease line.

Crease the fold, unfold, and pin over the crease.

5. At the pin, stop stitching with the needle in the fabric. Remove the pin. Turn the quilt ¼ turn and backstitch off the edge of the quilt.

6. Clip the threads, and remove the quilt from the machine. Move the binding straight back over the edge, and then bring it forward until the fold aligns with the quilt edge. The lengthwise folded edge should be flush with the fold under it; the raw edges should be flush with the edge of the quilt.

Align the raw edges with edge of quilt.

Begin stitching at the edge of the quilt and continue to the next corner. Repeat the corner procedure for the remaining three corners.

Join Beginning to End

The final joining seam of the binding should look exactly like the other binding seams when completed. I call my technique for doing this final angled seam "The Power of 1."

When you started the stitching, you left 8" of binding free. At the end, also leave about 8" unstitched. The two ends should overlap by at least 3".

1. Holding the 2 ends of the binding, find the center of the unstitched area. Insert a straight pin, perpendicular to the quilt edge. This will be the goal post.

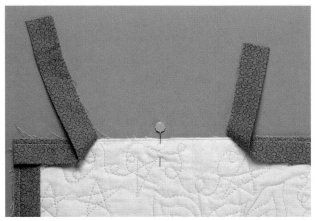

Goal post

2. Cut each side of the binding 1" beyond the goal post, leaving 2" of binding for the joining seam. To do this, move the left side of the binding out of the way, and position a small rotary cutting mat on the quilt to the left of the pin. Extend the right binding tail over the goal post pin. Place a rotary cutting ruler so that the 1" mark is directly on top of the pin and a horizontal line is on the ruler aligned with the quilt edge. Cut the binding at the left edge of the ruler. **Be very careful to have a rotary cutting mat between the binding and the quilt.**

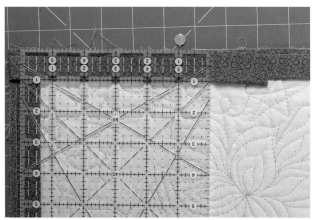

First cut

3. Repeat this process for the other side of the binding, extending the left binding tail to the right of the goal-post pin. **With a rotary mat between the quilt and the binding, cut the binding 1˝ beyond the pin.**

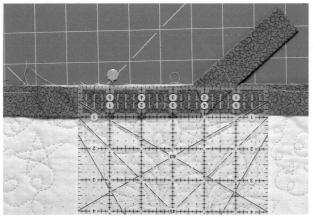

Second cut

4. With right sides together, fold one binding end over the other. Pin on all 4 corners. Draw a line from one corner to the other, as shown. Stitch on the drawn line.

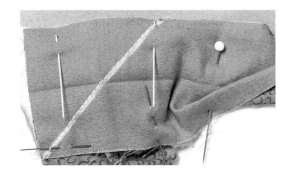

Mark the stitching line.

5. Before trimming the excess fabric, fold the binding and place it on the quilt edge. This will confirm that the seam was correctly stitched and will fit neatly on the quilt.

If no adjustment is needed, unfold the binding, trim the seam allowance to ¼˝, and press open.

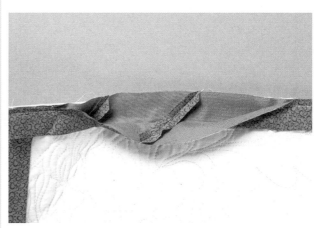

Trim and press seam open.

6. Stitch the remaining binding area to the quilt edges.

Stitch Binding to Back of Quilt

1. Fold the binding to the back of the quilt and hand stitch it in place, using thread to match the binding. When I use a cotton batting, I press the binding away from the top side of the quilt to make it easier to turn.

2. Use a blind hem stitch so the stitches will not show. At the corners, stitch the binding all the way to the edge of the quilt. Fold the binding over the next side of the quilt, forming a miter. The two sides of the binding should meet exactly at the 45° line. Stitch the miter on the back side of the quilt, then bring the needle through to the front. Stitch the miter in place on the front; this keeps it in alignment. Bring the needle to the back and continue stitching the binding to the quilt.

Lone Star Wallhangings

Gone Fishing, 38″ x 38″, machine pieced and quilted by the author.

To make smaller Elegant Lone Stars in a wallhanging size, a choice of two methods can be used. First determine what size block you wish to make based on the chart, then choose your cutting method. You can purchase new fabric or use fabric leftover from a larger Elegant Lone Star quilt.

✻ Wallhanging Sizing Chart

This chart will help identify templates to cut for a specific size wallhanging. Refer to page 17 for an explanation of the shapes to cut.

WALLHANGING SIZING CHART				
DESIRED SIZE	FINAL BLOCK	DIAMOND No Seam Allowance	SQUARE with Seam Allowance	TRIANGLE with Seam Allowance
45″	45¼″	13¼″	13¾″	20″
40″	40⅛″	11¾″	12¼″	17⅞″
35″	35″	10¼″	10¾″	15¾″
30″	30¾″	9″	9½″	14″
25″	25⅝″	7½″	8″	11⅞″
20″	20½″	6″	6½″	9¾″
15″	15⅜″	4½″	5″	7⅝″

✻ Materials

Lone Star block: 3 yards* (for fabric with a 24″ repeat)
Background: 15″, 20″ stars: ½ yard; 25″ star: 1 yard; 30″, 35″ stars: 1½ yards; 40″, 45″ stars: 2 yards
(It is difficult to give an exact amount due to variation in repeat size, both horizontally and vertically.)

✻ Cutting

METHOD 1: Cut Smaller Diamonds From Side to Side Repeats

As a general rule, there are 2 full and 1 partial horizontal repeats across the width of a fabric (see page 21). The design is rarely directly across from the same design on the other side of the fold, but is offset by half of the vertical repeat.

Vertical repeats in fabric

The width of the fabric will yield twice as many smaller diamonds as larger diamonds.

One source for wallhanging fabric is new focus fabric that has not been cut into. The amount of yardage, which is much less than what is needed for a bed quilt, depends on the number of identical cuts that can be made from the focus fabric. Count actual motifs in a particular fabric by placing the desired size diamond template over each motif.

Position of possible diamond cuts

Only 2 cuts can be made across the fabric, as the diamond on the right side extends off the fabric edge.

METHOD 2: Use Leftover Fabric for Diamond Cuts

Another source of fabric for wallhangings is to use the fabric leftover from the diamonds cut for a larger bed quilt. The diamonds will coordinate with the focus fabric in the quilt, and when used in the same room with the bed quilt the wallhanging amount will create a unified look. It is possible to cut diamonds for more than one wallhanging from the leftover fabric. The size of fabric between the large diamond cuts will limit the size of your diamonds for wallhangings. For this method, 6 yards of a 24″ repeat focus fabric is needed.

CUT DIAMONDS FOR BED QUILT FIRST

From the whimsical focus fabric on page 69, I cut diamonds for a 70″ Elegant Lone Star block.

70″ Block

CUT LEFTOVERS INTO MANY WALLHANGINGS

From the areas surrounding the large diamond cuts, diamonds were cut to make one 40″, one 35″, two 30″, and two 25″ small Elegant Lone Star blocks. Each of these can be the focus of a separate wall-hanging.

25″ block from leftovers

Template layout for 70″ block plus 6 wallhangings

Although this focus fabric had little change in design or coloration, each wallhanging block features a different design.

40″ block from leftovers

After the diamonds are cut, use the chart measurements to cut the background pieces. Follow the piecing directions in Chapter 5.

Finish the wallhanging by adding floater, pieced, appliquéd, straight, or other types of borders (see pages 49-55).

GONE FISHING
Finished Size: 38″ × 38″

Materials

Focus fabric (24″ repeat): 3 yards, or use leftovers from a full-size quilt

Royal blue background and borders: 1½ yards

Gold accent borders: ¼ yard

Binding: ⅜ yard

Pattern Piece Sizes

Star block: 30¾″

Diamond: 9″ without seam allowances

Squares: 9½″ with seam allowances

Triangles: 14″ baseline with seam allowances

Make diamond, square, and triangle templates from the pattern on the pullout, or following the instructions on pages 11–17.

Cutting

Focus fabric:

Center star: Cut 8 diamonds.

Royal Blue:

Background fabric: Cut 4 squares and 4 triangles.

Border: Cut 4 strips 1½″ x 35″. Cut 4 strips 2½″ x 40″.

Gold:

Border: Cut 4 strips 1¼″ by the width of the fabric.

Binding: Cut 5 strips 2″.

Quilt Assembly

1. Sew the diamonds, triangles, and squares into the star block following the sewing procedure for the large block (page 35).

2. Sew the gold accent border pieces between the 2 sizes of the royal blue strips to make 4 border sections. Add to the star block and miter the corners.

3. Quilt as desired. Bind to finish.

Small Eight-Pointed Stars

Angie's Stars, 85" x 99", machine pieced by Shirley Loose, hand quilted by Helen Crow. Using larger star blocks on the top and bottom of the quilt and smaller star blocks on the sides changes a square quilt to a rectangle.

Leftover focus fabric can be turned into small eight-pointed stars very easily. These stars add a wonderful touch to background areas and borders.

The sizes and shapes of these leftover areas will depend on how you position the original diamonds for cutting, and how large the diamonds were. After the large diamonds were cut for the model quilt in Chapter 5, the focus fabric looked like this.

Focus fabric with large diamonds removed

Each of the 4 edges around a diamond shares the exact same design area as in all of the other 7 diamond spaces.

✳ Determine Block Size

Diamonds can be cut any size, but some sizes are more "ruler friendly" than others. Template-free cutting can be used to cut diamonds, triangles, and squares for these 8-pointed star blocks, using measurements from the chart below. Another option is to use Ardco metal window templates, which are available from Quiltsmith, Ltd., for all sizes listed. Their edges are indestructible and easy to rotary cut around.

✳ Divide the Leftovers

Look at the areas around the holes left from the diamonds. If there is an area that is considerably smaller than the other areas, choose it to work with first. After cutting larger diamonds for another quilt from my focus fabric, a strip about 3½″ wide was left between each diamond.

Leftover fabric strip

Referring to the Small Stars Cutting Chart, the largest sizes that I could cut from leftover 3½″ strips would be either 3″ or 3⁵⁄₁₆″ strips, which makes either 12″ or 13¾″ star blocks. These sizes use almost all of the leftover strip width, with little waste. I chose to cut a 3″-wide strip so I would have ample fabric width to do a clean-up cut before making the diamond cuts.

SMALL STARS CUTTING CHART FOR 8 BLOCKS

FINISHED STAR SIZE	STRIP WIDTH	FINISHED SIDE OF DIAMOND	AMOUNT OF BACKGROUND	SQUARES: CUT 32	TRIANGLES: CUT 8 SQUARES
13¾″	3⁵⁄₁₆″ *	4″	1¼ yard	4½″	6⁷⁄₈″
12″	3″	3½″	1	4″	6¼″
10¼″	2⁵⁄₈″	3″	¾	3½″	5½″
8½″	2¼″	2½″	½	3″	4¾″
6″	1¾″	1¹³⁄₁₆″ *	¼	2⁵⁄₁₆″ *	3¾″

Note: Sixteenths of an inch are not marked on rotary rulers. The measurement of ⁵⁄₁₆″ is halfway between ¼ and ⅜″. The measurement of 1¹³⁄₁₆″ is halfway between ¾″ and ⅞″. Solution: Use a marker to temporarily add a small dot on the ruler where the sixteenth needs to be aligned.

WHERE IS STRIP NUMBER 8?

Remove the leftover strips from the focus fabric. There are 7 strips between the 8 diamond-shaped holes. Eight diamonds are needed to make an 8 pointed star, so another strip must be cut from the identical area next to either the first or last diamond cut from the focus fabric.

Place one strip on the identical area so the designs on 3 sides match and the strip seems to disappear. One side will be precut; cut the other 3 sides by laying a ruler over the cut strip on top.

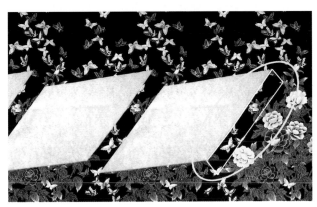

Find strip 8.

CUT THE DIAMONDS

Now you are ready to cut the strips into stacks of diamonds. Each stack will produce an individual block. Cutting and stacking the fabric strips into 8 per stack makes cutting the diamonds—all exactly the same size and same design—for smaller 8-pointed stars a very easy task. Each star will create its own new design.

STACK THE FABRIC FOR DIAMOND CUTS

1. Carefully stack the 8 pieces of fabric so the design in each strip is lined up exactly on top of the same design area.

2. After the 8 strips are layered, step back and look at the edges of the stack. If a strip is out of place

design-wise, it will show up on the cut edge when you are viewing the whole stack. Readjust the stack if necessary.

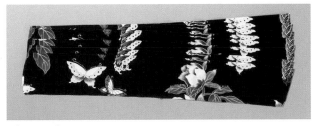

8-layer stack

TRIM STRIPS AND CUT THE DIAMONDS

1. Prior to cutting, pin the 8 layers together with flower-head pins to keep them in place. Do a clean-up cut along the long edge of the strips to make sure all the edges are straight.

2. Measuring from the clean-cut edge, cut an appropriate strip width based on the Small Stars Cutting Chart. For my stack, that width is 3˝.

> *tip* ALWAYS RECOUNT THE NUMBER OF FABRICS IN YOUR STACK BEFORE CONTINUING TO SUBCUT. BE SURE YOU HAVE 8 LAYERS IF YOU ARE PIECING FULL STARS, OR 4 LAYERS IF YOU ARE MAKING HALF STARS.

3. Place the ruler on the strip stack with the 45° line on the long edge of the strips. Cut the ends of the strips to establish the angle on one side of the diamond.

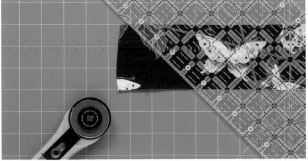

45° angle cut

4. Move the ruler so the 3″ line is on the angled end of the stack. This is the same measurement as the strip width. The 45° line should be on the long edge of the strips.

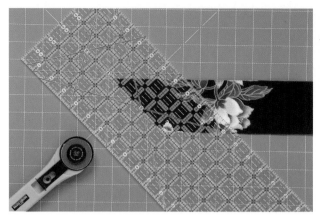

Ruler position for 3″ diamond cuts

5. Cut through all 8 layers, which yields diamonds for 1 block. Pin the cut stack of diamonds together—they are design-specific and must be used together to create a new design within a block.

6. Continue placing the 3″ line at the end of the strips, cutting until the entire stack has been cut. Now is a good time to take a peek at the cut blocks. From my 3½″ x 21″ leftover area, these 4 blocks were cut.

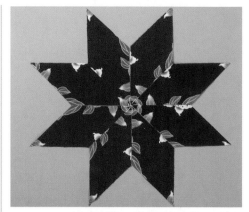

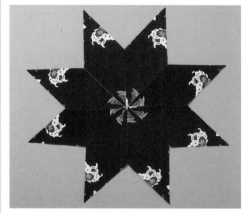

1st design option

If you turn the diamonds around, the 4 blocks would look like this.

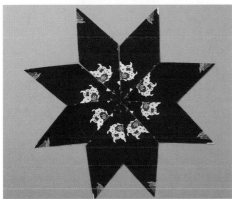

2nd design option

CUT THE BACKGROUND SQUARES AND TRIANGLES

Refer to the Small Star Cutting Chart to find the correct measurements for the 4 squares. For the 3"-wide strip just used, the diamond has a 3½" finished side. You need 4 squares 4" × 4" including seam allowance.

For the 4 triangles, cut 1 square 6¼" × 6¼", then cut the square across both diagonals. This places the straight of grain on 2 outside edges, and the crosswise grain on the other 2 outside edges. These triangles are much smaller than those used in the large block, which makes crosswise grain edges acceptable.

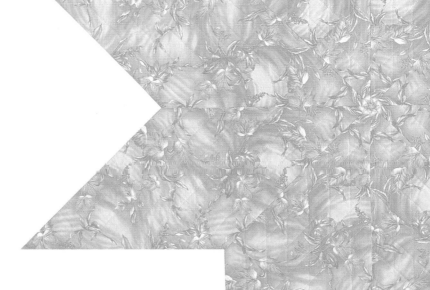

✳ More Stars

There are still 2 other areas you can use to cut more diamonds from your leftover focus fabric. Both of these areas have a selvage edge. If a few more star blocks are needed, consider cutting the smaller of the 2 areas next.

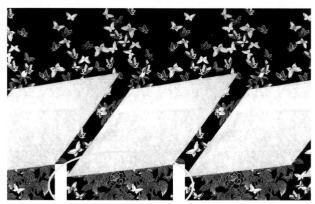

Second cutting area

This smaller area would be less useful in borders or other projects than the wider area. On my focus fabric, this measures 7½″ × 24″. Using a strip width of 3″, this area yields 2 strip stacks (3″ + 3″) from the 7½″ width.

An added advantage to using strips cut along the selvage edge is that the grainline will be on the straight of grain on 2 sides of the diamond. This area will yield another 8 star blocks, 4 from each strip stack. If more blocks are needed, the larger leftover area of focus fabric may be cut, stacked, and cut into diamonds.

Third cutting area

PIECE SMALL STARS

The small star block is pieced the same as the large star block, with one exception. No pinning is required except for the final center seam. The seams are short, so they do not cause the problem of stretching as in the large star. Follow the large star piecing instructions in Chapter 4.

Divide the Background with Pieced Blocks

Fantasia Night Star, 94″ x 94″, machine pieced and quilted by the author.

*I*nserting pieced eight-pointed star blocks into the large background squares and triangles provides interest and extends the design area.

Small Blocks and the Large Quilt Block

Inserting pieced blocks at the outside edge of the background adds the illusion of an inner pieced border within the block itself. A 13¾" block fits well within the background squares for a 70" block.

Pieced blocks are inserted in the background in *Fantasia Night Star* **(page 83)**

Template Drafting Shortcut

Use the pieced block and the background template to make new background templates.

1. Pin the pieced block in the corner of the square template, lining up the edges.

2. Draw lines on the template around the other 2 sides of the pieced block.

3. Draw a third line from the inside corner of the pieced block to the opposite corner of the template. (When drawing this line, position the 45° ruler line on the bottom edge of the template.) The original template is now divided into 3 pieces. Remove the pieced block.

Template divided into 3 new templates

ADD SEAM ALLOWANCES

The pieced is unfinished and includes seam allowances. When the lines were drawn around the block, they were drawn to this size. A ½" seam allowance must be added to the drawn lines.

1. For identification, use a red pencil. Draw a red line ½" away from the black line, on the side toward the block. This red line represents the cutting line for the trapezoid just drawn.

2. The line extending to the corner must also have seam allowances added. With the red pencil, add ¼" seam allowance to this line.

Both background pieces will be identical shapes, with one piece a mirror image of the other.

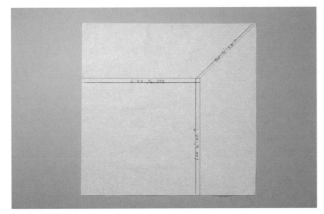

Add seam allowances.

3. Do not cut the original background template. Instead place a piece of Pattern Ease pattern making material over the "revised" template. Draw a new template for the trapezoid, following the red lines and the 2 outside template edges. Cut and label this template.

4. Cut 8 trapezoids, with 4 reversed (4 and 4R) for 4 blocks. Fold the background fabric wrong sides together; pin the trapezoid template with flat-head pins. Cut the 2 layers at the same time. The pieces will be mirror images to fit around the pieced block.

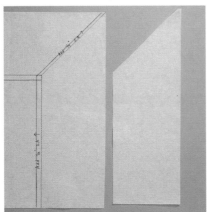

Trapezoid template

DIVISION OF THE TRIANGLE

The triangles are not as large as the squares, so a smaller 8-pointed star block must be used to provide proper proportion of scale. For a 70″ block, the 8½″ block fits nicely within the triangle and is visually pleasing.

1. Center and pin the pieced block on the long edge of the triangle template. Draw lines around the block. Remove the pieced block. Extend the line drawn at the bottom of the pieced block across the triangle, edge to edge.

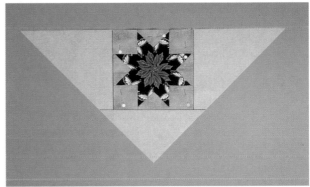

Division of triangle template

2. The original triangle template will now be divided into 4 pieces. The 3 pieces that will be cut from the background fabric are labeled 1, 1R, and 2. The outside edges of the original template have seam allowances included. Add ½″ seam allowance to Piece 1 with a red pencil. Add ½″ seam allowance to Piece 2, using a blue pencil.

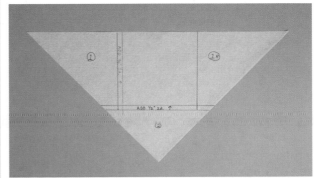

Add ½″ seam allowance.

3. Place a piece of pattern making material over the original triangle template. Draw the new pieces needed; label the side piece 1 and 1R. Cut 4 and 4R. Label the center piece 2. Cut 4.

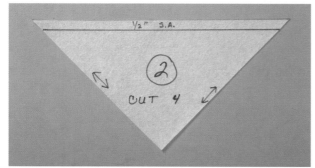

Two new templates

CENTER STARS WITHIN BACKGROUND AREAS

Follow the same process when centering stars within the background. Always add ½″ seam allowance if the seam is next to an "unfinished block measurement," and ¼″ seam allowance if the block is divided along any area not touching the pieced block.

ALTERNATE METHOD FOR DRAWING TEMPLATES

Graph paper can also be used to draft the templates. Draw the "finished" size of the pieced block. Complete the division lines. Add seam allowances and prepare new templates. If you are using this method, ¼″ seam allowance is used to enlarge all the templates because the "finished" size of the pieced block was used instead of the "unfinished" size, as in the previous shortcut instructions. This method is very difficult if the pieced block is a size not easily identified on graph paper lines, such as the 13.7″ block used above.

Ivory Stampede, 90″ x 90″, machine pieced and quilted by Shirley Stutz.

FANTASIA NIGHT STAR

Finished Size: 95″ × 95″

Materials

Focus fabric (24″ repeat): 6 yards
Black background and border: 6 yards
Binding: ⅔ yard

Pattern Piece Sizes

Star block: 85⅜″
Diamond: 25″ without seam allowances
Squares: 25½″ with seam allowances
Triangles: 36⅝″ baseline with seam allowances
Make diamond, square, and triangle templates.

Cutting

Focus fabric:
Center star: Cut 8 large diamonds.
Small stars (12″): Cut 8 pieces approximately 4″ × 25″. Stack and cut 3″ wide. Cut one end at a 45° angle. Measure from the angled end and subcut at 3″ to make 4 stacks of 8 diamonds each.

Small stars (8½″): Cut 8 pieces approximately 3″ × 18″. Stack and cut 2¼″ wide. Cut one end at a 45° angle. Measure from the angled end and subcut at 2¼″ to make 4 stacks of 8 diamonds each.

Background fabric:
Borders: Cut 4 pieces 5½″ × 98″ (includes extra in length) on the lengthwise grain.
Small stars (12″): Cut 16 squares 4″ × 4″. Cut 4 squares 6¼″ and cut diagonally to make 16 triangles.
Small stars (8½″): Cut 16 squares 3″ × 3″. Cut 4 squares 4¾″ × 4¾″ and cut diagonally to make 16 triangles.
Binding: Cut 11 strips 2″ × width of fabric.

Quilt Assembly

1. Following the same procedure as for the Elegant Lone Star, make four small 8½″ stars and four small 12″ stars.

2. Draw the templates for the large background pieces by placing the 12″ star on the square template and the 8½″ star on the triangle template. Follow the Template Drafting Shortcut directions (page 80).

3. For the squares, cut 8 trapezoids with 4 reversed (4 and 4R).

For the triangles, cut 8 side pieces with 4 reversed (4 and 4R) and 4 center pieces.

4. Sew the background pieces to the small stars. Press toward the background fabric.

5. Sew the diamonds and background pieces into the star block.

6. Add the black border pieces. Miter the corners.

7. Quilt as desired. Bind to finish.

Broderie Perse Appliqué

Flower Power, 92″ x 92″, machine pieced by the author, machine quilted by Vickie Yanik.

ome elements in large fabric designs are good choices for Broderie Perse appliqué. Bringing parts of the focus fabric out into background areas adds visual appeal to the Elegant Lone Star quilt. Look for areas in the focus fabric that have smooth edges in the design for ease of appliqué. Multiple parts can be cut out and arranged together, or just one area can be cut, which considerably reduces the time required to do the appliqué stitching.

Shortcut Appliqué Preparation

Using fusible web on the edges of Broderie Perse appliqué is a good method of preparation. It is quick and easy to apply and helps eliminate any frayed edges when edges are not turned under. A disadvantage of using fusible web to glue the applied fabric in place is the stiffness that may result if the web is applied over the entire appliquéd area. It is more desirable to add fusible web only around the edges of the applied piece.

1. Cut a fusible web product, such as Wonder Under, in ½" strips across the width of the fusible sheet.

2. Rough cut the chosen fabric design area, a minimum of ¼" beyond the desired design edge.

Cut out the fabric design.

3. Using an appliqué pressing sheet to protect your ironing board, place the design on the pressing sheet, wrong side up.

4. The fabric edges follow a design line in the focus fabric. Tear off small pieces of the fusible strip to cover the design line. Place the pieces, paper side up, on the wrong side of the design fabric, covering the edge. Iron baste in place—just touch the tip of the iron to a spot on the fusible strips.

Baste fusible web to fabric.

This will hold the little pieces of fusible web in place until the entire design can be pressed. Proceed around the design, adding little pieces of fusible web strips until the outer edge of the design is covered. Do NOT skip any of the fabric on the outside edge. Cover with an appliqué pressing sheet to protect the iron from any fusible web that may have separated from the paper backing. Press in place, following the manufacturer's directions for the fusible product you are using. The time required to hold the iron in place varies with each product.

tip ANY FUSIBLE WEB THAT STUCK TO THE APPLIQUÉ PRESSING SHEET CAN BE REMOVED WITH A SMALL PIECE OF COTTON BATTING. CLEAN THE PRESSING SHEET AFTER EACH PIECE TO PREVENT ANY OF THE GLUE FROM FUSING TO THE RIGHT SIDE OF THE NEXT APPLIQUÉ.

5. Let the fabric cool completely. Remove the paper backing. Cut to the exact design line desired. Cutting the design after removing the paper eliminates any fraying that might occur in paper removal. The appliqué is now ready to be attached to the background. The fused area should look cloudy compared to the color of the remainder of the fabric. The fabric should now have approximately ¼″ of fusible web around the entire design.

Press appliqué in place.

6. Stitch the appliqué piece in place. Several methods are acceptable. A decorative stitch on your sewing machine can be used. One stitch that adds a beautiful finished edge is the blanket stitch, sometimes referred to as a buttonhole stitch. A matching or contrasting thread may be chosen, depending on the look desired. Rayon thread, size 30, provides good coverage on the edge, and prevents any possible fraying.

Blanket stitch

Invisible appliqué is another good choice. Use .004 monofilament thread, or a thread that matches the color of the applied piece. Because the edges are not turned under, the width of the stitch needs to be wide enough to prevent the needle from raveling the fabric edges during stitching. Generally, a width of 1.5 is desirable. The length of the stitch needs to be close enough to prevent raveling and result in a well-adhered appliqué. A stitch length of 1.0 usually provides good coverage.

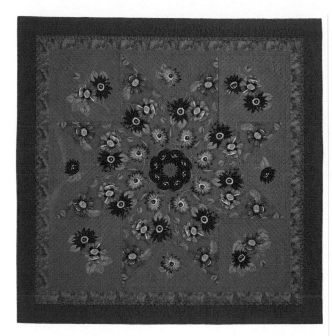

FLOWER POWER

Finished Size: 92″ × 92″

Materials

Focus fabric (24″ repeat): 6 yards

Brown background and floater border: 4¼ yards

Light blue border: 1¼ yards

Coral border: 1¼ yards

Medium blue border: 2¾ yards

Binding: ⅔ yard

Fusible web: 1 yard

Pattern Piece Sizes

Star block: 70⅞″

Diamond: 20¾″ without seam allowances

Square: 21¼″ with seam allowances

Triangle: 30⅝″ baseline with seam allowances

Make diamond, square, and triangle templates.

Cutting

Focus fabric:

Center star: Cut 8 diamonds.

Appliqué: Cut 4 large and 4 medium motifs.

Brown:

Floater border: Cut 4 lengthwise grain pieces 2″ × 76″.

Background pieces: Cut 4 squares and 4 triangles.

Light blue:

Border: Cut 8 pieces 3½″ wide × the length of the fabric.

Coral:

Border: Cut 8 pieces 1½″ × the length of the fabric.

Medium blue:

Border: Cut 4 pieces 6″ wide × the length of the fabric.

Binding: Cut 10 strips 2″.

Quilt Assembly

1. Assemble the diamonds, triangles, and squares into the star block (page 35-44).

2. From the leftover focus fabric, select and cut 4 larger motifs for the background squares and 4 medium motifs for the background triangles. Prepare the back of the motifs with strips of fusible web (page 85). Trim, then fuse to the background pieces. Stitch the appliqué motifs in place.

3. Piece the light blue pieces and the coral pieces to make 4 borders of each fabric. Sew to the floater border and the medium blue borders. Add to the quilt and miter the corners.

4. Quilt as desired and bind to finish.

Reverse Appliqué

Flowering Urns, 96″ x 96″, machine pieced and quilted by the author.

✳ Window-Framed Appliqué

Reverse appliqué embellishment, using design elements from the focus fabric, substantially alters the appearance of the background. You can use different shapes, such as an oval, circle, diamond, triangle, or square, to cut a window from the background. You can also use a large design from the focus fabric to create an interesting shape. Trace shapes on the back of the background fabric, then cut a window opening on the marked line.

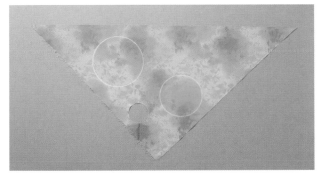

Cut openings on marked line.

DRAW AROUND "FOUND" DESIGN

Move the focus fabric under the openings to look for the best image. Mark around the "found" motif at the edge of the opening. Also make orientation marks on both the background and the motif at clock positions of 3, 6, 9, and 12. This will help in positioning the cutout design.

Mark the motif.

ADD SEAM ALLOWANCE

Cut the motif ½" larger than the markings to allow for an ample seam allowance. The same motif can be repeated by moving the piece around on the focus fabric until the design lines match. Many different motifs from the focus fabric can also be used.

PREPARE FOR APPLIQUÉ

1. Apply fusible web to the wrong side of the window opening in the background fabric. Cut ½" strips of fusible web.

2. Working on an appliqué pressing sheet, position the background fabric with the wrong side up. Cut the fusible strips into shorter lengths, from 1" to 3".

3. Place the pieces with the paper side up.

4. "Iron baste" by touching the tip of the iron to each short strip around the entire edge of the opening. The fusible web will extend slightly over the edge. This basting will hold the fusible web in place until the whole area has been covered. Be sure to cover the entire edge.

5. To protect the iron from unwanted glue, cover the fabric with an appliqué pressing sheet. Follow the manufacturer's directions for the time needed to press the fusible strips in place.

6. After the fabric is cool, remove the paper. Turn the fabric to the front and trim the excess fusible web from the edge. Position the focus fabric motif behind the opening and line up the orientation marks. Cover with the pressing sheet, according to the manufacturer's directions.

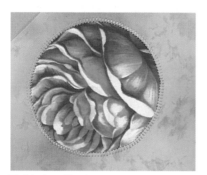

Finished appliqué

APPLIQUÉ IN PLACE

Use thread to either match or contrast the color of the background fabric. Either a blanket stitch or invisible machine stitch is appropriate for appliquéing the design in place. The advantage of doing reverse appliqué over regular appliqué is the ease of thread matching. Usually a design from the focus fabric contains multiple colors, so matching the thread to this fabric is difficult. Most backgrounds are less varied in coloration and easier to match thread color. Rayon thread, 30 or 40 weight, gives good edge coverage with a blanket stitch. Rayon also adds a nice sheen. If an invisible stitch is used, either monofilament .004, or a cotton $60_{1/2}$ thread in a matching color are good choices.

A more formal look can be achieved by inserting identical images from the focus fabric, as shown in *Flowering Urns.*

Formal placement of reverse appliqué

FLOWERING URNS

Finished Size: 96″ × 96″

❋ Materials

Focus fabric (24″ repeat): 6 yards
Rose background: 5¼ yards
Tan border: 1⅓ yards
Maroon border: 1½ yards
Binding: ¾ yard
Fusible web: 1 yard

❋ Pattern Piece Sizes

Star block: 85⅜″
Diamond: 25″ without seam allowances
Squares: 25½″ with seam allowances
Triangle: 36⅝″ baseline with seam allowances
Make diamond, square, and triangle templates.

❋ Cutting

Focus fabric:
Center star: Cut 8 diamonds.
Reverse appliqué: Cut 4 motifs.
Rose:
Background: Cut 4 squares and 4 triangles.
Tan:
Border: Cut 8 pieces 2″ wide by the length of the fabric.
Maroon:
Border: Cut 8 pieces 4¼″ wide by the length of the fabric.
Binding: Cut 11 strips 2″.

❋ Quilt Assembly

1. Assemble the diamonds, triangles, and squares into the star block (pages 35-44).

2. Cut openings in the background pieces that match a design element in the focus fabric. Prepare the back of the background edges with strips of fusible web (see page 85). Fuse and stitch in place (page 86).

3. Piece the tan and maroon pieces to make 4 borders of each. Add to the quilt and miter the corners.

4. Quilt as desired and bind to finish.

Embellish the Star

Happiness . . . Is Color, 94″ x 94″, machine pieced and quilted by the author.

In spite of careful fabric selection, the central star sometimes has a "mushy" look. Some reasons for this are print designs that are too similar in scale, similar colorations and/or values, and too little resting area between elements. These may cause failure to produce easily identifiable new circular designs. You can rescue the inner design by isolating a wreath of flowers (or other design element) and separating that area from the outer part of the star with an appliqué.

Some Fabrics Need Extra Help

My quilt *Happiness...Is Color* is a prime example of a beautiful floral print that contained multiple colors and shapes of different sizes, but too little resting area between the elements. When the diamonds were all cut and placed on the design wall, only the blue in the center and the next ring of flowers contributed to any new design. Beyond that, there were some lovely flowers that all looked like mush or like the fabric as it came off the bolt.

Because I loved the coloration of the beautiful flowers, I was not willing to settle for the mediocre. Instead, I wanted to find a way to magnify the third wreath, which had a combination of all the beautiful flowers in the fabric. Since this wreath was located just inside the widest part of the diamond, I designed a swag type of appliqué. Using a Pattern Ease diamond template on top of the fabric diamond, I drew the outline of the swag. Using that line as a base, I drew feathers, side by side, to fill the area directly beyond the wreath of flowers.

BRIGHT FABRIC INTENSIFIES DIVISION OF STAR

To further isolate the wreath of flowers, I chose the bright chartreuse fabric. This fabric provided an intensely colored separation between the wreath and the outer part of the star. I cut out the fabric and prepared it with fusible web on the edges. I then fused it to the fabric diamond and appliquéd it in place prior to piecing the star block. (See page 85 for preparation of appliqué.)

BONUS QUILTING PATTERN

An added bonus to using the Pattern Ease for the pattern was that it also became the quilting pattern for this area. Leaving the top and bottom of the feathers intact, the lines between the feathers were cut so a marking pencil could be used to mark the quilting lines.

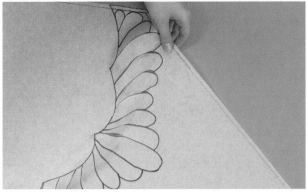
Innovative quilting stencil

An ineffective design rescued by addition of appliqué

FABRIC DICTATES THE DESIGN

Because each fabric design is different, any appliqué you add to isolate a wreath would need to be personalized to the way the design elements are arranged in the fabric. A smooth curving line is often appropriate.

To determine a swag shape, place the diamond template on top of the fabric diamond and roughly establish the outer edge of the design to be featured by drawing on the template with a pencil. Draw only half of the swag, fold the pattern in half, and trace the first half to the other side for an exact mirror image.

WHEN TO APPLIQUÉ

The swag can be appliquéd prior to piecing the block, as in my quilt. An alternate method would be to include the ends of the swag in the side seams of the star, and appliqué the other edges in place after the big block is pieced.

HAPPINESS... IS COLOR

Finished Size: 94″ × 94″

Materials

Focus fabric (24″ repeat): 6 yards

Orange background fabric: 2½ yards

Green background and border fabric: 4¼ yards

Navy border: 1⅓ yards

Binding: ¾ yard

Fusible web: 2 yards

 Pattern Piece Sizes

Star block: 80¼″

Diamond: 23½″ without seam allowances

Triangle: 34½″ baseline with seam allowances

Make diamond and triangle templates.

Cutting

Focus fabric:

Center star: Cut 8 diamonds.

Reverse appliqué: Cut various motifs.

Orange:

Cut 8 triangles.

Green:

Border: Cut 4 lengthwise grain pieces 6″ x 98″ (includes extra in length).

Background: Cut 4 triangles (place short sides on grain.

Appliqué: Cut 8 swags or other shapes.

Navy:

Border: Cut 8 pieces 2″ wide by the length of the fabric.

Binding: Cut 10 strips 2″.

Quilt Assembly

1. Cut openings in the green background triangles. Prepare the back of the openings with fusible strips (see page 85). Place over the focus fabric motifs. Fuse and stitch in place (page 86).

2. Sew the appliquéd green triangles to 4 orange background triangles. Sew the diamonds, triangles, and squares into the star block.

3. Piece the navy pieces to make 4 borders. Sew to the green strips to make 4 border pieces. Sew to the quilt and miter the corners.

4. Quilt as desired. Bind to finish.

About the Author

Shirley Stutz lives on a farm in beautiful rural southeastern Ohio with her husband, Loran. Her first quilt, begun in 1985, took three years to make. Using the methods of yesteryear, she found the process so slow and tedious that she declared that since she now had a new quilt for the bed this would be her last quilt. When rotary cutters were introduced, her love for making quilts quickly grew. As guilds and shops saw her work, requests began to surface for her to teach quilting classes.

She began teaching patchwork in 1990 and now is a full-time traveling teacher, including two trips to Germany. Her goal is to inspire students with innovative faster methods, without sacrificing accuracy. Her five machine-quilting classes remain her most popular year after year. She says happiness is seeing the light go on as a student embraces and understands a new concept (and visits from any of her nine grandchildren).

Shirley is much in demand for her humorous lectures, which always include a mini-lesson on topic and a trunk overflowing with quilt examples.

She enjoys entering one or two national shows each year, with several quilts now ribbon winners. The Amish quilting community in Berlin, Ohio, honored Shirley in 2002 when she was asked to display 117 quilts in a solo exhibition, which attracted several thousand visitors.

Several of her quilts have been published in quilting books and magazines, including *Borders and Other Finishing Touches* by Bonnie Browning; *Award Winning Quilts and Their Makers*, AQS; cover and featured Artist, *Quilt Ohio, American Quilter,* and *NQA Quilting Quarterly*. Her pattern, Feathered Fantasy, was one of the Collector Series by Craftco, Inc.

Sources

The six products mentioned in Chapter 3 can be found at many quilt shops; they are also available by mail order from:

Townsquare Fabrics
7 Tiber Way
Marietta, Ohio 45750
(877) 373-6150
Email: info@townsquarefabrics.com
Website:
http://townsquarefabrics.com

Metal Window Templates
Quiltsmith
252 Cedar Road
Poquoson, Va 23662-2112
(800) 982-7326
Email: sales@ardcotemplates.com
Website: www.ardcotemplates.com

For more information about C&T books, ask for a free catalog:
C&T Publishing, Inc.
P.O. Box 1456
Lafayette, CA 94549
(800) 284-1114
Email: ctinfo@ctpub.com
Website: www.ctpub.com

For quilting supplies:

Cotton Patch Mail Order
3405 Hall Lane, Dept. CTB
Lafayette, CA 94549
(800) 833-4418
(925) 283-7883
Email: quiltusa@yahoo.com
Website: www.quiltusa.com

Note: Fabrics used in the quilts shown may not be currently available because fabric manufacturers keep most fabrics in print for only a short time.

Index